FAITHFUL

THE ROBERT AND ELEANOR PALMER STORY

Robert E Palmer

Eleanor Palmer

FAITHFUL

THE
ROBERT AND ELEANOR PALMER
STORY

ROBERT E. PALMER
WITH ELEANOR M. PALMER

❈ FOREWORD BY T. RAY RACHELS ❈

2017
PALMER PRESS

SANTA MARIA, CALIFORNIA

Palmer Press
1189 Foxenwood Drive
Santa Maria, California 93455

Editor: Susan Palmer Marshall
Associate Editor and Image Editor: Paul E. Palmer
Copy Editor: Scoti Domeij
Cover and Interior Designer: Heather Wood
www.HeatherWoodBooks.com

ISBN 978–069–28612–19

Printed in the United States of America
1   3   5   7   9   10   8   6   4   2
First Edition

To the memory of our parents
Jessie and Hattie Palmer
&
Clarence and Vera Gardner
Who taught us to walk in His way,

And to our children, grandchildren, and
Great-grandchildren who inspire us
Each and every day.

Acknowledgements

There are people who surely influenced us
by their words and examples, besides our parents.
Among them, Rev. Howard Osgood, a missionary, who took
a great interest in and challenged me to live totally for Jesus.

Pastor Henry Hoar, with whom we worked for four years
as young, inexperienced ministers. By his example and words he
taught us so much about being a pastor and how to respond
to the ministry of the Holy Spirit in the services.

The many godly teachers at Central Bible Institute in Springfield,
Missouri, who added so much to our lives.

We also want to thank those who assisted in the writing of our
book: Mary Robinson, who read the first draft.

Our children, Paul and Phyllis, who provided insights into their lives.

Roger Simpson, who helped me with the technology
to keep from losing all I wrote.

Heather Wood, who designed this book
so beautifully and thoughtfully.

Scoti Domeji, who provided gracious and meticulous copyediting,
and, finally, to Susan Palmer Marshall, my grandniece,
for her invaluable assistance in reading, editing and preparing
the manuscript for publication. She has been a real blessing to us.

CONTENTS

FOREWORD

When I finished reading the manuscript of *Faithful: The Robert and Eleanor Palmer Story*, I sank back in my chair, closed my eyes briefly, and inhaled nostalgic memories of two of the finest people I know. The principal thing I recognize about Bob and Eleanor is this: If you want a living representation of integrity, faithfulness, honor, ministerial loyalty, and a description of the meaning of "Christ-follower," you need to look no further than these two wonderful servants of the Lord. It has been my privilege to call them friends since 1976, when we were pastoral colleagues in greater Los Angeles. Bob's elder brother, Leonard who he talks about so warmly in the book, and I were neighboring pastors in Long Beach, while Bob and Eleanor led a great congregation, Del Aire Assembly, in nearby Hawthorne. I can only hope and pray that any congregation would be so blessed to have a "Palmer," like these, as their leaders and spiritual shepherds.

The book took me on a journey of … *And God did it …* the book's regular thematic sections, giving notice about the Palmers' recognition of God's sovereign hand that pointed them forward, always forward, into His ever unfolding plan for their lives. It reminded me of the Psalmist's word "Selah," which regularly directs the reader to pause and remember that it was the Lord who has brought us this far. What a great autobiographical story. And they finish their story with "… each of us is in our ninetieth year … but we remain on the firing line for the Lord." That sounds so much like what I would expect them to say.

Bless you, my dear friends, for your lives of servanthood. And, may we all embrace such wise counsel.

—T. Ray Rachels
Southwest Area General Council Executive Presbyter, 2011–present
Southern California District Superintendent, 1988–2010
Assemblies of God

INTRODUCTION

This is the true story of two young people who as children felt the call of God to serve the Lord with all their hearts. Both have tried to be faithful to the Lord as first children, then teenagers and, finally, adults. They prepared themselves by reading God's Word and being in prayer constantly while they were in high school and then at the Central Bible Institute. It is a remarkable story of how the Lord has led their lives and blessed their ministries both in the United States and overseas.

Any and all of the incidents recorded in this book are not for boasting, but rather to illustrate what God can do if people will follow His leading in their everyday lives.

This is our story ... the story of our families, of our coming together as a couple, and of our collective lives in service to Him.

And now, to all of our children, grandchildren, great-grandchildren, nieces, nephews, friends, and whomever else may read this story of God's goodness. We want to meet each of you in the place prepared by the Lord for all of us who will follow Him. Don't put it off, don't hesitate, but make peace with God now and be sure your name is in the Book of Life.

To God be *all* the Glory.

—ROBERT E. PALMER AND ELEANOR M. PALMER

PART 1

ROBERT'S STORY

And God did it.

It was Sunday morning on April 17, 1927, and things began to get exciting around the home of Jesse and Hattie Palmer in Burlingame, Kansas. Their children consisted of Stephen Leonard, 19, a student at Central Bible Institute (CBI) in Springfield, Missouri; Margaret Elizabeth, 17, a senior at Burlingame High School; Dwight Ervin, 15, a sophomore at Burlingame High School; and Paul Eugene, a toddler at three years old. This was no ordinary Sunday; it was Easter Sunday morning. But it was also the day that a new voice was heard in the form of a son, Robert "Bobby" Earl Palmer (me), who made his entrance into the world at the Palmer house on Dayton Avenue. I don't really remember anything about that day, but I do know that I was born into a loving home. My Mother, Harriet "Hattie" May Thompson Palmer, was 42 years old and on May 4, 1927 celebrated her 43rd birthday. My Dad, Jesse Ervin Palmer, was also 42, and on September 29 of that same year celebrated his 43rd birthday.

Dad left the farm near Franklin, Nebraska in 1922 to become a carpenter and a lay minister and moved the family to Burlingame, Kansas. Both Mother and Dad became Pentecostals in the early days of the Pentecostal Movement before the Assemblies of God was formed. They attended T. K. Leonard's Gospel School in Findlay, Ohio, circa 1914, and both received ministerial credentials with the Assemblies of God. When the family moved to Burlingame they built a church and parsonage and, after some time, secured a minister to pastor the church.

I remember being in that building several times as a child. It had Celotex (insulation board) on the walls, and Bible verses printed on the front walls. It was not a large building, but adequate for the times. Though my parents were both 42 when I was born, I never felt that they were older people. In fact, my Mother sometimes traveled with my brother, Leonard, many years later when, as a District Official, he preached, and she looked so young that some people thought she was his wife.

My Dad, Jesse Palmer, was a good man; an avid searcher of the Word of God; and one of the hardest-working men I have ever known. I wish that I could have worked with him for two or three years as a carpenter. He was always busy. I remember him having a Ford Model T truck with a pulley attachment to the rear wheel. He used this to cut firewood. There was a large round saw blade attached by a long canvas belt to the pulley. Dad was quite an experienced finish carpenter, and he could do more with a hand saw than many could with table saws. He also used all kinds of electrical tools for his work, which I found fascinating. He had a large garden and sometimes a cow. During World War II, Dad helped to build the Fort Riley and Topeka Army Airbases. I never heard him ever use a curse word. His worst expression was "Confound that confounded thing."

I remember our family altar and when he prayed, "So teach us to number our days that we may apply our hearts unto wisdom," before closing the prayer. I also recall once after our prayer time Dad apologizing to Mother for something he had said to her. I have never forgotten his humility in doing that. I wish that my kids had known their grandfather, Jesse Palmer. Unfortunately for all of us, he went to be with the Lord in 1953 at the young age of 68 due to complications of falling and breaking his hip. A blood clot had formed and traveled to a vital organ. Medical treatments were not as advanced back then as they are today.

As the youngest member of the Palmer family, I suppose I was highly favored by my parents. (At least my brothers thought I was.) Leonard and Dwight agreed that my parents were easier on me than on them. One thing I do know, I lived in a house where I was loved by them all.

My brother, Leonard, and C. M. Ward—the great preacher on Revivaltime Radio—had married sisters Esther Deane and Dorothy Mae Hymes, in a double wedding on Christmas Day, 1929 (which was shortly after their graduation from CBI). Leonard became a pastor in Western Kansas for several years and then at Ottawa, Kansas. It was there that Esther Deane died, leaving two young children—Dorothy Deane and Jack

Ervin—who came and lived with us for several months. I really enjoyed having them live with us, and have always felt like they were more like my younger sister and brother, than my niece and nephew.

I remember once I gave Jack a ride in a wagon and turned too short. The wagon tipped over and he broke his arm. I felt so badly about that accident.

Leonard left the church in Ottawa and later became a pastor in Kansas City. He then married Frieda Maxine Steinle, an evangelist in her own right, and they soon travelled together as evangelists prior to becoming pastors in Miles City, Montana. After pastoring there for several years, Leonard was elected to the position of District Superintendent of the Assemblies of God-Montana District. While in that position they were called to Brisbane, Australia, to be pastors of Glad Tidings Tabernacle, now Brisbane City Church. Leonard was also very involved in the Australian Assemblies of God. After returning from Australia they became pastors at Three Cities Assembly in Burlingame, California. Later he became the Assistant Superintendent and Superintendent of the Northern California District of the Assemblies of God (AG). During their relocation in cities and employment, Leonard and Frieda had three daughters together, Gloria Lee (born in Miles City), Joy Dawn (born in Brisbane) and Robyn Lynn (born in Burlingame). Their next pastorates were in Fairfield, Taft, South Gate and Long Beach, California. Leonard also was Chaplain at Beverly Hills Doctors Hospital. At age 86, he still served as visitation pastor at First Assembly in Fairfield when he died. Leonard was a great man of God.

I was very attached to my sister, Margaret, who was almost like a second mother to me. Upon meeting Earl Bond, a classmate of my brother Leonard's at CBI, Margaret fell in love, and they soon made plans to get married. After their marriage, Margaret and Earl began their pastoral ministry in the state of Ohio, followed by pastorates in two different cities in Indiana. I didn't get to see them very often because they lived so far away. Margaret and Earl had three girls: Earlene Marie, Louise Elaine, and Esther Ruth.

Sadly, Earl died at the age of 43 while he was District Superintendent of the Assemblies of God in Ohio. He had previously served as the Secretary-Treasurer, and later as the Assistant Superintendent of the Central District (Michigan, Indiana, and Ohio) of the Assemblies of God. Shortly thereafter, Margaret and the girls moved to Northern California, and she became Secretary to Leonard when he was the Assistant Superintendent and Superintendent. Later, Margaret continued serving as a secretary to other officers in the Northern California District until her retirement. She was a widow for 52 years, and died at the age of 92. Earlene passed away in 2006; Louise and Esther both live in the Santa Cruz, California area. Mother relocated to Santa Cruz in 1956 after Dad had died. She and Margaret lived together at their home in Bethany Park for 23 years until Mother passed away in 1979. I always appreciated Margaret so much for caring for our mother.

My brother, Dwight, was dating Alice Ardelle Ward, and she was so sweet to me. He often brought her to our house, and I really loved her. I imagine I was something of a pest as a little kid, but they seemed to like having me around. They married and lived in Burlingame, Kansas, too, so I got to know them better than Leonard and Margaret. When our house burned down in 1937 or 1938 we moved to the upstairs of their house while Dad rebuilt our house. For a time, Dwight and Ardelle tried farming on the farm my parents still owned in the state of Nebraska, but they couldn't make it financially. The last place I remember them living in Burlingame was just up the street from where I lived until I was 16. It was in 1942 that they moved to California, then ten years later, to Oregon.

Dwight and Ardelle had two daughters, Helen Margaret and Mary Charlene. They were beautiful young women and both actively served their country. Helen Chenoweth-Hage became a member of Congress from Idaho and served as a Republican for three terms in that office. Charlene served in the Peace Corps and was also a captain in the U.S. Army. In August 2006, Charlene died of cancer and, just two months later, Helen was killed in a tragic highway accident.

I don't really remember much about my earliest years, but I do have a faint memory of running down the street with my brother Dwight chasing after me when I was quite small. At the wedding of my sister, Margaret, I was four years old, and went to sleep. The wedding was held at our house in Burlingame, Kansas. I didn't want Earl to marry Margaret because I loved her so much and thought that I would grow up to marry her. She was around until I was four years old. Truly, I was a blessed child to be born into such a loving and godly home. From my earliest days, I can remember going to church. My brother, Paul, and I played together, even in church, and

I remember at least one time that Mother separated us while the service was going on in Scranton, Kansas, where she was the pastor.

We lived in Burlingame, Kansas, a typical Midwestern town, the kind of place where everyone knew everyone else. In those days, there was no kindergarten, so I went directly to the first grade at Schuyler School—about two blocks from home—and attended there for the first four grades. I am told that I was afraid I wouldn't know anything when I went to school, so I had my Mother teach me some basic things (counting, ABC's, etc.). When I came home after the first day and was asked about it, I replied, "I already knew everything the teacher taught us today."

When I was seven, my Mother and I went to Pratt, Kansas, to stay with Leonard, and his wife, Esther Deane, who was ill. I remember it so well because Leonard was the pastor at the church in Pratt where I gave my heart to the Lord and began my spiritual journey that continues to this day. While there, we attended a meeting that displayed different Bibles sponsored by the American Bible Society. Among them was a small New Testament with individual books and a little plastic case in which to put the book that one was currently reading. I begged Mother to buy it for me (which she did), and I had it for many years. I never did read it through, though. It was only after I made a rededication of my heart to the Lord at age 15 that I began to devour the Word of God.

When I was age seven and Paul was age ten, we began delivering the *Kansas City Star* and *Times*. We got up at 5:00 a.m. and delivered the *Times* and, in the evening, the *Star*. We delivered a paper 13 times in a week to customers and were paid three cents per customer from the owner of the route, which gave us some spending money for our efforts. We didn't have to collect from the customers directly. It was important that we learned to work with such dedication that early in life.

Paul and I were very close. He was my big brother and took care of me. He taught me to ride a bike while I was quite young. I had an old bike with an iron seat and no padding on it. Right after I learned to ride, we rode for some distance to the country to see some friends. I was afraid to ride over a bridge, so I hopped off and pushed the bike across, and then Paul pushed the bike to get me started again. He was very patient with me that day.

I was quite a daredevil back then. We had a rope swing attached up high in one of the elm trees in our side yard, and I climbed a tall ladder to catch hold of the gunny sack filled with old clothes or other sacks and then swung down. It was enjoyable, and we spent many hours playing there. We also had much fun in the wintertime going down the hill on our sleds. It seemed that the snow was quite a bit deeper when I was a child than when I got older.

The following reveals that God had a purpose for my life. I was a very foolish kid sometimes. When I was little, I found some shotgun shells and rifle bullets in the kitchen pantry. So, I took them outside to a rock in the garden and tried to hit the cap with a hammer to see what would happen. Had I succeeded, I could have been seriously injured. Another time when I was 10 or 11, I found a cigarette lighter on the street somewhere. I flicked the lighter and it sparked, but nothing happened. I decided that it needed some lighter fluid. Since no one in our house smoked, we had no lighter fluid. Then I remembered Dad had a five-gallon can of gasoline in the basement. I went downstairs and tried to pour gasoline into the tiny hole on the lighter. Of course, when I flicked it this time, it lit the gasoline on my hands and the floor, which jumped up to the can. Fortunately, I had put the cork back into the gasoline can. I don't know how I did it but I picked up the burning five-gallon can, took it to the basement door, and threw it into the yard where it burned out. Many things could have happened that day. Our house could have burned down and, had it exploded, I would have been seriously burned or killed.

But God had a plan.

When I was nine, a great tragedy happened in our family. My brother, Paul, who I looked up to with such regard was found drowned. He went to a swimming pool in Osage City with the young people from the Presbyterian church. The group got ready to leave and Paul was not with everyone else. No one knew how his death happened. Paul didn't know how to swim, but his body was found in the deep water. We were told that one lifeguard left the pool before the next one arrived, so it might have been neglect on the part of the pool staff.

I don't remember much about that sad time. But I do remember that his body was brought to the house and was laid upon the bed. I seem to recall that Dad asked Mother, "Should we pray for the Lord to raise him up?"

She said, "No."

This was a very difficult time for all of us, but especially for Mother.

Shortly after his death, I quit delivering the Kansas City newspaper. Feeling quite devastated, I needed the time to deal with my loss of Paul. It was as if my mind shut down regarding him. Because of suffering this kind of loss at such a young age, I can hardly remember him at all.

When some appropriate time had passed, I began delivering the *Kansas City Journal*, the *Wichita Beacon*, and the *Topeka State Journal*—all at the same time. After two or three years, I became the paperboy for the *Topeka Daily Capital* and delivered it until we moved to Michigan when I was 16. Since it was the largest newspaper route in the area, it gave me a lot more spending money.

When I was 14, I got my driver's license. This gave me the ability to drive with my parents' permission and in the daytime only. Even before getting a license, I loved cars. I would back up our old 1929 Dodge out of the garage and drive it back in again. However, after getting my license, I could drive on my paper route or almost anywhere. Later, I had a 1930 Model A Ford coupe. Today it would be worth a lot of money. Just before we moved to Michigan I had a 1923 Model T Ford Coupe, which had belonged to a kid at Kansas State College in Manhattan. He put 16-inch wheels on it, painted it many colors of the rainbow with a sponge, and changed the hood to open like a more modern car. I paid $50.00 for it and sold it before moving to Michigan for the great price of $35.00. I still have a picture on the wall in my office of me standing by it.

We always attended church services regularly. In those days

it was still legal to have Bible classes in public schools, so my Mother was involved in teaching one of the classes. Mother was well known in the town and was sometimes called upon to conduct funerals, as well as preach in the church. Some of my earliest remembrances of church were in the Scranton Assembly of God where Mother had become the pastor. I only remember one couple from that congregation. They were Swedish and invited us to their home for Sunday dinners. I never drank coffee except at their house. It was so good, but it probably had a lot of cream and sugar in it to make it taste that way.

When Mother quit being the pastor at Scranton, we started attending the Baptist church in Burlingame, Kansas, and continued to worship there until we moved to Michigan in 1943. We went to Sunday School, morning service, Baptist Young People's Union and Sunday evening service every Sunday. But going to church that often didn't make me a Christian. I had to accept Christ personally, as I related earlier. We, as Christians, often need to rededicate ourselves to the Lord.

In October of 1942, we went to a revival meeting at the Topeka First Assembly of God, about 30 miles from Burlingame. Evangelist Gene Martin preached a powerful sermon on the rapture of the Church and what would happen to you if you were left behind. Venita Dunn, a classmate and friend, and I went to the altar call that night. Venita and I were both born on the same day, and we are friends to this day. I spoke with her recently, and she still remembers that night. It was the beginning of my rededication of my life to Christ, but I didn't start growing in the Lord until May of 1943.

As soon as school was out in 1943, my Mother and I left for Grass Lake, Michigan, where Dad had accepted a position as Caretaker/Manager for FA-HO-LO Park—the Assemblies of God camp meeting grounds. The name stands for "Faith, Hope, and Love." At that time, we had a 1941 Plymouth. The gas ration board allowed us gas stamps for only 60 gallons of gas. Mother and I drove the whole trip from Kansas to Nebraska and then on to Grass Lake, Michigan, at 35 miles an hour, and averaged 25 miles per gallon. It was a great trip. We went to Nebraska to take my Aunt there, and then we drove on through Iowa, Illinois, and into Michigan to Grass Lake. I loved to drive, and this was the longest trip on which I'd ever been the driver. To this day I still like to drive, except in slow traffic in the Los Angeles or San Francisco areas.

On May 30th, our first Sunday there, we attended church at the Jackson Assembly of God in Jackson, Michigan. The pastor of the church was Arden Ragsdale, a very fine man. He and his wife were there for several years. The church building was an upstairs hall on Michigan Avenue that was used for Bingo on Saturday nights and church on Sundays. That morning in the service, I confess that I had observed a couple of young ladies who were really worshiping the Lord. I was impressed by their attitude and their looks, as I was a sixteen-year-old guy. When the altar call was given, I went forward with the rest of the congregation and began from that day to live a life for Christ in earnest. My life was changed as I began to read the Word of God and pray daily.

To this day, I still think about going up to the altar with everyone else to pray—not in response to a call for sinners—

but as was the custom in those days of everyone going forward. Perhaps today, people might be saved or rededicated in the same manner if offered the opportunity, just as we were that Sunday. I try to remember this when I preach and give an invitation. It is much easier for someone to come forward to accept Christ or make a dedication of one's life if others also come to the altar, rather than going up alone.

In June of 1943, there was a National Youth Conference at Central Bible Institute in Springfield, Missouri. Since I had just rededicated my life on May 30th, I wanted to go to the conference. I didn't have much money, and neither did my parents. As it so happened, I was driving down the private drive to the camp grounds one day, when a fox ran in front of me, and was hit and killed by the car. I discovered that there was a bounty for killing one so I received about $25.00 for the pelt. I was sorry for the fox, but delighted that this accidental killing made it possible for me to go to the conference without financial difficulty. Arrangements were made, and I enjoyed ten wonderful days at the conference and was challenged to live completely for the Lord. At one of the first services, I was filled with the Holy Spirit and began to know what it meant to live for Christ. The speakers at that conference were really great and offered much advice about how to live a Christian life.

Rev. Howard Osgood, a missionary to China, also gave us some advice about our future. He said that we should pray for our future wife or husband and to be very specific about it. He said that when he became a Christian he began to pray for the girl who would eventually become his wife. He asked the

Lord that she be saved, filled with the Holy Spirit, called to the ministry, and also called to be a missionary. He went to China single, but found that the answer to his prayer was already over there as a missionary.

So, I began praying the same way. I prayed for a wife who could play the piano, sing alto, and love me. I will tell you a little later how God answered my prayer. I met some young people at the Youth Conference who became good friends a year later when I went to CBI to study for the ministry. I came back from that conference filled with the Holy Spirit, on fire for God, and determined to live for Christ.

I preached my first sermon that Christmas at the Jackson Assembly of God. I still remember the topic "Behold the Lamb of God." I'm sure that it was not a profound message. In the year that I spent in high school in Grass Lake I persuaded a few of my classmates to come to church with me—some of whom were saved. I hope that they are still going on with God. I know that a girl, one of my friends from Grass Lake High School, later married a widower from the Jackson AG Church.

I took some business classes that year which included typing, shorthand and bookkeeping. Two of these were useful at CBI and during my 72 years of ministry. I used shorthand only once, and that was to write a letter to Eleanor. She had to have someone else read it for her. I sure wouldn't be able to use that ability now.

I also worked afternoons and Saturdays at a small factory in Grass Lake during my year in high school there. I learned a lot while working in the factory. I learned not to complain about the work I was asked to do and, if I did a good job, I'd be promoted. First, I did cleanup, put putty in window frames, and other menial tasks. Being a typical teenager, I wanted to run drill presses. However, the boss called me in and explained that what I was doing was important. If I didn't do it, then he would then have to have an experienced machine operator do it and that would slow up the war work we were doing. Properly rebuked, I went back to work a lot harder and smarter than before.

It wasn't long before I was given the job of driving a 1940 Ford pickup loaded with parts to be taken to Jackson to be heat treated. That I enjoyed and, later on, I got to run drill presses, too. We all (and that included me) have a lot to learn if we are going to get along well in this world. I have often said, "Do more that you are expected to do, and soon you'll have a better job and often make more money." When I left the job to go to Central Bible Institute to study for the ministry, the boss gave me a bonus equal to a semester at the college. Praise the Lord.

The camp meeting was held each summer at FA-HO-LO Park, and the dates for the meeting usually included the weekend of July 4th. Often during those war years, the camp attendance reached up to 3,000 on that weekend. Originally, they erected a large tent for the services. A year or two after Dad arrived, plans were made to erect a large metal tabernacle. I think it was 100 feet by 300 feet without any posts on the inside so there was no obstruction in front of anyone. Because of his experience in building, Dad was a very valuable man to have there at that time. They always had outstanding Assembly of God speakers, and we had camp meeting. Dad and Mother were very involved, as Dad was the caretaker. If anything didn't work, it was his job to fix it. Mother worked long hours in the dining hall and kitchen preparing food and serving the people. As a potential minister of the Gospel, they both were good role models for me.

In the summer of 1944, before my freshman year at Central Bible Institute, I was again in contact with Rev. Howard Osgood, who had prayed with me the night I had received the baptism of the Holy Spirit. He offered some very good advice. He said, "Bob, I hope while you are at CBI, you will see your way clear to be cordial to all of the young ladies, but friendly to none of them until your senior year at least." That was very good advice, because I was only 17 years old when I went to CBI. Many of the young people met someone and fell in love just as soon as they got to school. I followed that advice and never did seriously date anyone during my three years at school.

That fall, I enrolled as a new student at Central Bible Institute in Springfield, Missouri. What a blessing that was to me. I learned so many things at CBI during those years. Some of our classes were Old and New Testament, personal evangelism, English, word study, prophecy, and doctrine, as well as other basic classes which were needful for those who were preparing for ministry. Though tuition was only $100.00 per semester, we also worked 12 hours per week for our room and board.

During my first year, I washed pots and pans as my job. In my second year, I worked in the mimeograph room with Raymond T. Brock, who later became a missionary to Africa and a teacher at Evangel University. I learned so much preparing classroom notes and how to use various kinds of equipment. That experience proved to be one of the best things that I learned at CBI, as I was my own secretary for my first years as a pastor. In my third year, I was the business manager on the staff of the college annual, *The Cup*. It was a very busy time, but I learned so much working with Floyd Woodworth, editor of *The Cup*, and his future wife Millie Zoppelt, who was the literary editor. They became missionaries to Cuba and, eventually, to all of Latin America. They were good friends for many years.

We also studied hard. Every morning, we attended chapel services. Daily at noon, there was the Missionary Prayer Band where we prayed for missions. On Friday nights, the whole evening was given over to worship, and the Word was spoken by a faculty member or a guest speaker such as a District Official, a General Council leader, and sometimes even by a former student who was a pastor, evangelist, or missionary. We were constantly challenged to be what the Lord wanted us to become. How I thank God for those years of training at CBI.

Dormitory life was tough because we usually lived in rather cramped quarters: a small room with a single bed, bunk beds and a desk. My three years at CBI were a growing experience for me and, no doubt, for all of the students who were willing to learn and adjust to the fact that others also have rights. One of my roommates, Fenton Jones, used to say, "Living so close is like sandpaper."

Another of the great things we learned at CBI was to be sensitive to the Holy Spirit of God. One night I remember that two or three of us felt burdened to pray. We went down to the prayer room, but we didn't know what to pray about. None of us felt any particular matter on our hearts. After a short time someone said, "Maybe the devil is just trying to keep us from the sleep we need." So, we prayed, "Lord, show us what to pray about or remove this feeling." Immediately it left, and we went back to bed free of what we now know was the enemy trying to rob us of sleep. At Central Bible Institute there were great times of spiritual revival that resulted in countless young people becoming missionaries to foreign lands. We also developed numerous friends throughout these many years that remained close to us.

During my first year at CBI, I became a part of the student ministry outreach. This meant that we went to "outstations" (places of ministry) in towns around the Springfield area, and conducted services in schoolhouses, vacant church buildings and/or rented facilities. Many of those places now are Assembly of God churches. I went with a group going to Reeds Spring. We held services in a meeting hall above a garage, my first real pulpit. During that year we were able to see some people come and at least one young man was saved. He later became the Youth Leader of a local Free Pentecostal Church in Reeds Spring. It was a learning experience for all of us "kids" from CBI. Each of us had the opportunity to preach, to lead the singing, to play an instrument, to pray with people, and to do visitation outreach. During those afternoons of visitation I met some people that challenged me. Especially those who said their church was the only one that was right and that we were wrong. Of course we didn't agree with that. It was a good learning experience for us. We learned to lead in those outstation services. Many of us became pastors and missionaries to foreign lands as well Bible college teachers, and local members of churches.

In the summer of 1945, I became the leader of a small group in Galena. The lady Rev. Opal Pogue, who had been the pastor, became a missionary to Africa, and that began my ministry there. For two years while I was in CBI, and for two-and-one-half years after my graduation, I pastored the Galena Assembly of God. I was very young—only 18—when I became a pastor. I had so much to learn, and those days were just what I needed to develop a sense of responsibility, and to become a person who really cared about people.

That was 72 years ago, but I still remember the few who gathered in the earlier days. We met part of the time in the peoples' homes and part of the time in rented buildings. Finally, we met in a corrugated steel warehouse donated by a local businessman with a 20-foot by 30-foot room for the church meeting place. He was very gracious to allow us to use it for two or three years. It was very rustic to say the least. The building had no water and no bathroom. A filling station down the street below the railroad tracks was available. The seats were 4-inch or 6-inch boards with an inch between each board and an almost straight-up back. But it was ours to use. It was on the main street of Galena, just down from the courthouse. As I recall, we had no rent and no electric bill. We must have had a heating stove for the winter months, but at least we had a home.

Most Sundays during my three years at CBI were spent in outstation work where we learned to be ministers. There would always be at least three of us students who went to outstation to conduct services. As I said, we took turns in leading the singing, playing an instrument, singing a solo, and preaching in the service. Sometimes all of us were very inexperienced. I remember once when one of the speakers said, "And the blood shall be turned into moon," when it was supposed to be "the moon shall be turned into blood." All the people and students broke into laughter. Our decorum was not good that particular day. But, we learned many things in those years at CBI and going to outstation. One thing we learned not to do was: Don't go eat your lunch in a field. There were ticks, little bugs that bite, in the pasture. That day they were all over us, and we had no place to go to change clothes and shower until we got home. Fortunately, none of us became ill from the ticks. This was way before Lyme disease. The showers were welcome in the dorms when we got home. Those were great days, and I made many good friends among the students who helped me in those two years prior to my graduation in 1947. Today, there are churches all over the areas near Springfield because of the students who were able and willing to become a member of an outstation group.

After my graduation from CBI in 1947, I moved to Galena, Missouri. I had no place to live and no church members could provide a place for me. I moved into a boarding house run by Mrs. Mathis. It was very good accommodations with wonderful food three times a day—including lots of fried chicken and all the fixings—all for only $15.00 per week. A dentist, a preacher (me), and two schoolteachers all boarded there. I enjoyed living in this fashion as a single young man as it was an ideal place to live.

Mrs. Mathis also took in men on some weekends who came to Galena to "float down" the James River to fish. They came from Kansas City and St. Louis for these "float" trips. Mrs. Mathis was always very careful to call on me to pray over the food. However, on the first occasion the men were there, they started filling their plates without the prayer and started to eat. I thought, *I must pray now or I never will pray over the food when they're here.* So I said rather loudly, "Don't you think we should thank God for all of this good food?" I didn't wait for their response; I just started giving thanks to God for the food. From then on, no matter who was there, I was asked to pray before we ate. I greatly appreciated Mrs. Mathis and the others who lived there.

Galena was—and is—a small town. It is the county seat of Stone County. The town was built around the square with the courthouse in the center. There were four churches—Presbyterian, Christian, Fundamental Baptist, and Assembly of God. The Presbyterians had no pastor, so on some Sundays several of the congregants visited us in the small sanctuary just above the tracks. It was always nice to see the seats well filled when they attended. I am thankful for the two-and-a-half years that I lived in Galena. I tried my best to minister to all those who lived in the area.

To support myself, I began to work at the courthouse, which afforded me contact with quite a number of the people in town. We once had a week of meetings on the corner of the square on a vacant lot. We moved the furniture out of the little building, seats, piano, pulpit and all, for an open-air revival. One of the young women from CBI, Juanita Gray, had become an evangelist, and she came and did the preaching. There was some interest because some people didn't believe in women preachers. So, one night she preached on "Should A Woman Preach?"

I am happy to say that today in Galena there is a very beautiful Assembly of God church in its own building right on the highway. I cannot take credit for what is there today because after I left other students came and contributed their efforts to building a congregation. Eventually, a pastor came and pastored there for more than twenty years during which time a very nice church building was built and the congregation grew; many of who are still there now.

In 2015, we visited the church on a Sunday morning and met the present pastor and the small congregation. It's always a joy to return to a church where you used to be the pastor to see what God has done. But God met us in the years that we were there from the summer of 1945 until Thanksgiving of 1949. It's the best looking church in Galena, and one of the most attractive buildings in the whole town.

One night in February of 1949 I decided to drive over to Crane Assembly to see our friends Ted and Evelyn Vibbert, who became pastors there while Ted finished his last two years at CBI. Evelyn was in the class of 1947 and Ted was in the class of 1949. One of the students from CBI, Ed Lack, was conducting a revival meeting for them. They needed a pianist one night and had asked Eleanor Gardner to come with them to play the piano for the revival. That happened to be the night I went to the meeting. I noticed Eleanor playing but didn't remember her name. Later, one of the ladies from my church who was at the meeting said to me, "Eleanor would make you a nice wife."

Two nights later, I went back to the revival and she was playing the piano. I became interested and asked some questions about her of the other students who were there. I asked Ed Lack to come home with me Friday night, and on Saturday, February 12th, I took him to Springfield to CBI and inquired where I could find Eleanor Gardner. She was working in the dining room (her duty) and someone sent for her. When she came in the school office, I went over to her and asked if she would like to go out for lunch. I wanted to be very careful to not lead her on and then decide she was not the right one.

As we dated, I became keenly aware that she was the answer to my prayers and felt perfectly comfortable in her presence. I held her hand and once kissed her hand. A date or two later, I drove to the side of the girls' dorm and kissed her on the lips then took her to her door.

From then on we both knew we were destined for each other. Those next few months passed by quickly and the great day of our marriage arrived. I stood there waiting for Eleanor and her Dad to come down the aisle, and she stopped at the archway in the center of the aisle. Floyd played "I Love You Truly," and I sang the song to my beautiful bride.

That was the beginning of the love story of Eleanor Gardner and Robert Palmer.

PART 2

ELEANOR'S STORY

My dad, Clarence Gardner, was an orphan. His mother had died when he was quite young. His father was a doctor, but for some reason Dad had found himself on his own at an early age. A family named Gardner took him in and he adopted their name as his. No one seemed to know if he had any siblings or other relatives. It's all a bit of a mystery. Dad met Vera Pfleeger, my mother, before he left for the military in World War I, and upon his return they married. Seven children were born to this union.

I came into this world on September 11, 1927, as Eleanor Maxine Gardner at 1412 South Campbell Street, Springfield, Missouri. Prior to my birth, Mother had dedicated me to the service of the Lord. I was the first daughter and the third child of seven born to this hardworking couple. Leonard Clarence was born in 1920; Eugene Victor in 1923; Virginia Mae in 1929; Charles Edward in 1932; Jack Howard in 1933; and Jean Darlene was born in 1938, but died as an infant of three months. One night, a drunken driver killed Eugene, about age twelve, as he walked home after being uptown. This was a traumatic experience for our family, which caused us to draw even closer to the Lord.

My brother Leonard was in the United States Army during World War II, and upon returning home became employed at the Gospel Publishing House in the Printing Department as a typesetter where he worked until his retirement. His wife Ruth also worked at the GPH, but in the Business Department until her retirement. Virginia worked at the GHP in the Home Missions Department for 14 years; Charles worked at the GPH for a short time, but later was in sales for Allstate Insurance. He married Anita who also worked at the GPH in the Home Missions Department for many years; Jack went into the Navy during the Korean conflict and, upon returning moved to St. Louis, he married Ruthie Tasch from Bethel Temple church. Ruthie's primary work was and is being a homemaker. Jack worked in construction as the superintendent of a sheet metal construction company that specialized in large projects.

Later, my family began attending an independent church built by the Brooks family who were Assemblies of God ministers. Mrs. Clara Brooks, known as "Cousin Clara," became the writer of a column for *Gospel Gleaners*, an adult Sunday School paper of the Assemblies of God. Her column was called *Cousin Clara Says*. The Brooks family were pastors of the church for several years, and were a great help to our family. I remember that they came to our house in a big black car and brought over groceries, as our family was poor. Later, Rev. and Mrs. Brooks retired and sold the church building to Rev. Floyd Hitchcock, a local independent radio preacher. I became close friends with Betty Hitchcock, the pastor's daughter, who was an inspiration to me. Our Sunday School teacher was Sister Hogan, the mother of Phil Hogan who later became the National Foreign Missions Director of the Assemblies of God.

I can remember that from an early age, I had a great desire to serve the Lord and to play the piano. Upon learning that I wanted to learn to play, a local pastor's wife gave me free piano lessons for one year. Because my family had no piano, I went to the teacher's house to practice every day for an hour, with a metronome no less. At the end of the lessons I could play two hymns: "Jesus Lover of My Soul" and "Wonderful Words of Life." Little did that dear lady who gave me those lessons realize what a blessing that young girl would become because she could play the piano.

Later, Mother bought me an old upright piano, and I learned to read music. I would go through the hymnbook and play every song in it. This is how I became so familiar with so many hymns. My friend Betty also taught me how to transpose music from one key to another. This ability was very important throughout our ministry. I also learned to play the accordion for the church orchestra.

My conscience is quite sensitive, and the following story reveals my sensitivity to the Lord and to others. When I was in grade school, the father of one of my female classmates was in the hospital. We all took up some money to give to his daughter to buy flowers for him. I was carrying the money, and we were downtown on our way home and passed by the Catholic church. We went inside and all the children except for me paid a little money to light a candle. I had no money and wanted to light a candle like all the rest, so I took two cents out of the flower money and lit a candle. Years later, while I was in high school and after I became a Christian, I felt very convicted about the two cents I took. I didn't know how to reach the girl because she'd moved away, and I had no contact with her for a long time. I had read an article by "Cousin Clara" in which she wrote, "Let Go and Let God." So, I told the Lord, "If I can get in contact with this young lady, I'll give the money to her but I don't know where she is. I put it into your hands and let go and let God." Shortly after this prayer, I received a letter from this girl who had never written to me before. She lived in California and I lived in Missouri. So, I wrote to her, attached the two cents, and witnessed to her about the Lord. My anxiety was gone immediately because God answered prayer with this miracle. Strangely, though, I never heard from her again.

When I was a young teen, a guest preacher spoke at a non-denominational church on the subject, "Lazarus, Come Forth," then asked for people who wanted to accept Christ as their Savior to come to the front and shake hands with the preacher. I went forward and shook his hand—but that's all that happened right then. When I went to bed that night, however, *something great happened*. As I began to pray, I felt the presence of Jesus and I was born again. I saw a wonderful, great, bright, and glorious light. My life was changed from that day forward. I will never forget that night.

Later on, our family began attending Southside Assembly in Springfield. I was in my teens and almost immediately began to play the piano for the church services. I felt inadequate because the students who attended the church were accomplished musicians. I sat in the congregation but Pastor E. K. Ramsay kept calling me to the piano, and the Lord helped me to conquer my fears and self-doubt. I continued to play there through my CBI years and until Bob and I were married.

When I was a junior in high school, it was announced that we could work half days and get credit toward our graduation. At first, I thought about getting a job at the dime store, but then I lay in bed and suddenly the thought came to me, *Why don't I try to get a job at the Gospel Publishing House?* Pastor Ramsay was head of the Printing Department, so I asked him about applying there. He told me to come in and submit an application, which I did. I turned sixteen on a Saturday and went to work on the following Monday for half days. This was a miracle in my life for the future. I worked with a lot of Pentecostal people, as well as missionaries and ministers. I worked there for three years—from age sixteen to nineteen. I also worked at GPH in the summertime between semesters. I loved the GPH because I was working for the Lord, as well as working at a paying job.

As a part of my preparation for ministry, I had a great desire to go to CBI and study, so I enrolled at Central Bible Institute in the fall of 1946. This was the beginning of the fulfillment of my dreams. I paid my way through CBI while working at the GPH. From the time I was a little girl picking up coal along the railroad tracks, I had a desire to marry a minister and serve

God in His Church. The three years spent at CBI, I was living in the girls' dorm; singing in the choir for the "Sermons in Song" national radio broadcast, later known as "Revivaltime;" listening to great preachers and teachers; sharing in the times of revival as the Holy Spirit flowed over and through us (classes would be dismissed while the Holy Spirit dealt with our hearts and lives); meeting new friends who are still friends today; and preparing my heart to love and serve God in a greater way. I loved Central Bible Institute then, and I do to this day.

I still remember the day a fellow student came over to the dining room at CBI and said to me, "Someone wants you in the office." I thought, *What have I done that I am being called to the office?* I didn't realize it was Saturday and that no one would be in the office. When I came into the lobby, Bob Palmer stepped up and said, "I'm the one who wanted to see you. Would you like to go out for lunch?" I went back to my room and got ready to go on a real date with a man who'd studied to be a preacher. In just a few minutes, we were on our way.

As we were going out of the campus, we looked up at the balcony where several of my friends stood watching. They ducked down, but we saw them anyway as we drove out. Our first date had begun. We went downtown to a hotel to eat our lunch and then Bob brought me back to CBI. Was I excited? You know I was. It was February 12, 1949, and that was the beginning of our six months of dating that led to our marriage on August 30th. Most of our dates were attending the Sectional Fellowship Meetings of the Assemblies of God in the Springfield area.

I remember the time Bob first kissed me on the lips and

walked me to my door. When I went inside one of my roommates said, "Someone has just been kissed."

I guess my face must have been glowing.

Bob worked fulltime in the courthouse, served as pastor in Galena and, at the same time, conducted a nightly revival meeting for seven weeks in Reeds Spring. One night, Virginia and I drove down to the meeting in a Model A Ford belonging to my brothers, Charles and Jack. I had wave clamps in my hair and forgot to take them out, which was an embarrassing moment for me.

There were about 27 young people who gave their hearts to Christ during those seven weeks, and 20 were baptized in water in the James River at Galena. After we moved to California years later, a young lady, a wife of a pastor, came up to me at Camp Pinecrest and asked, "Are you married to Bob Palmer from Springfield?"

I replied, "Yes."

She said, "I went to the revival he conducted in Reeds Spring and was saved there." She went on to say, "I had a crush on Bob and also came to your wedding."

Since August 30, 1949, I have been Bob's wife, pianist, organist, accordion player, choir director, and friend, as well as a loving mother to our children, grandchildren and great-grandchildren. We've had a wonderful partnership through these 67 years.

Now, back to Bob and on to our story.

PART 3

OUR STORY

Chapter 1

✦

Courtship

Prior to our marriage, while I was pastor at Galena, I worked in the courthouse to make a living. At first, I was a secretary to the County Superintendent of Schools and was paid $50.00 per month. After that, I became the secretary to the County Farm Agent and made $90.00 per month. Just before our marriage, I became a caseworker for the Welfare Department, now called Social Services, for which I received $150.00 per month, plus $.05 per mile for driving my car. I enjoyed working in the courthouse because I met people all the time. I also used the skills I had learned while working in the mimeograph room and as a member of the annual staff at CBI. Both Eleanor and I have learned through the years that each job or position that we have had in life has further prepared us for the next one.

As we dated for those six months we learned more about each other and were ready to make a lifetime commitment to one another. On June 12th, I asked, "Do you want to marry a preacher?"

She replied, "Yes."

Since I thought she meant me, I "hocked," meaning pawned, my cornet to get some money to buy her an engagement ring. On June 18th, we took her Dad uptown, and while he went into a store, I gave Eleanor the ring. When her Dad came back to the car, I held Eleanor's hand over the back of the front seat and asked, "Is this ok with you?"

Mr. Gardner smiled and said, "If she can live with it, I can live by it."

So, we were officially engaged. What a great deal this was for me, and she says the same. Eleanor's only complaint? It didn't happen before graduation so she could show off her ring to her friends. It was certainly a "match made in Heaven," because we continue to love each other more as the years go by.

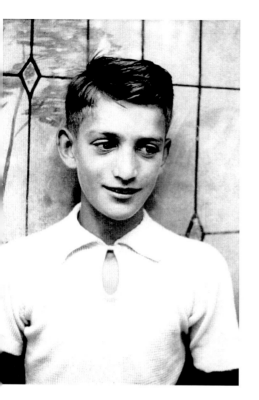

clockwise from top, left: Robert Palmer, age 14; Eleanor Gardner, age 13; Sisters Eleanor and Virginia Gardner; Brothers Paul and Robert Palmer

clockwise from top, left: Robert's family: Parents Hattie and Jesse with Robert and pet dog; Hattie and Jesse with Jack and Dorothy Deane Palmer (more like Robert's siblings than niece and nephew), 1937; Brother Leonard, Dorothy Mae Hymes Ward, Esther Deane Hymes Palmer, and C.M. Ward, December 1929; *back row:* Ardelle & Dwight, parents Jesse and Hattie, Earl and Margaret Bond, *front row:* Paul, Robert, and cousin Earlene Bond, c. 1936

top: Eleanor's family, *back row:* Virginia, Vera (in rear), Eleanor, Leonard (in uniform), and Clarence, *front row:* Jack and Charles; *bottom:* The Gardners near the railroad tracks where they picked up coal to heat their home during The Great Depression

top: The bicycle Robert used for his paper route; *bottom:* The Gardner family, *back row:* Robert Palmer, Charles, Anita, Virginia, Ruth, Leonard, *front row:* Eleanor, Vera (mother), Paul, Clarence (father), LaTheresha, Jack

clockwise from top, left: Eleanor with her portable keyboard, the accordian; Robert, age 15, with his 1923 Model T Ford Coupe; The Palmer family: Earl (Jesse's brother), Hattie, Margaret, Leonard, Dwight, Eleanor, and Robert on the occasion of Jesse's funeral, Canton, OH, April 1953

clockwise from top: Robert's first pulpit in the Outstation ministry meeting hall above a garage, Reed Springs, MO, 1945; Outstation ministry team in Reed Springs, MO, 1945; Reed Springs Pentecostal Church, c.1945; Eleanor, late 1940s

top:
The formal
wedding party;
right:
A ceremonial photo
of Robert and Eleanor
cutting the wedding cake
as husband and wife,
August 30, 1949

top: Eleanor's family's church, Southside Assembly of God, Springfield, MO, where Robert and Eleanor were married; *bottom:* Exiting the church after the wedding

CHAPTER 2

⟡

What God Hath Joined Together

Prior to our wedding, our many friends in Galena—the whole community as well as the congregation of the Church—gave us a shower. It was really a blessing to us, and we received many gifts as well as good wishes. The ladies of Southside AG also gave Eleanor a personal shower, which outfitted her for a long time with many beautiful things, and the people of Southside Assembly presented us with wedding gifts too. After all these 67 years, we still have some of those gifts. Rev. Howard Osgood, my friend and mentor before the wedding, and his wife, Edith gave us one of our most treasured gifts which we still cherish to this day. It's a Chinese tapestry embroidered with lovebirds, and a message of love in Chinese. It hangs above the computer in my office and it remains beautiful after sixty-seven years.

My parents still lived in Michigan at FA-HO-LO Park, and the summer season was the busy time of the year for the camps, so we had to set our wedding date for August 30th to give them time to come to Springfield for the ceremony. Our friends from Southside Assembly and Central Bible College were participants in the wedding. Rev. David Hastie was the officiating pastor; Rev. Floyd Woodworth, pianist; Rev. Harry Myers and Mrs. David Hastie were the soloists; Rev. Wayne Danner, Best Man; Virginia Gardner, Maid of Honor; Ruth Gardner, Bridesmaid; Leonard Gardner, Groomsman; Leila Clements, Bridesmaid; Rev. Anthony Palma, Groomsman; Willow Fuqua, Bridesmaid; J. D. Woody, Groomsman; La-Theresha Gardner, Flower Girl; and Philip Hastie, Ringbearer. What a great group of friends and family these people were.

Following the reception, Wayne Danner chauffeured us in his car to the motel on Glenstone Boulevard where we had a room reserved for our first night as a married couple. Someone had put Limburger cheese on the manifold of Wayne's car and had jacked up the back wheels from the ground, but we got to our destination safely. Our car was hidden at the motel, or it would have been our car that had been messed with.

The ladies of Southside Assembly provided the wedding decorations and the reception afterward. Eleanor and I were both thrilled that Rev. W. I. Evans, Dean of Central Bible Institute came to our wedding. Our mutual friends filled the sanctuary at Southside where Eleanor had served as the pianist so faithfully for many years. Pastor and Mrs. David Hastie were such good examples of those in ministry. Eleanor tried to pattern her life in ministry after the example of Mrs. Hastie.

Following our wedding, we spent the next day driving in our 1935 Ford to Grass Lake, Michigan, to spend our Honeymoon in my parent's home. My parents were babysitting my sister's children in Canton, Ohio, while Earl and Margaret Bond went to the General Council Meeting in the Northwest, so that worked out well for us to have a week in Michigan. Upon our return to our little apartment in Galena, we began our married life together in our own home. You should have seen us trying to buy groceries by ourselves in Springfield before the return trip. You would have laughed as we tried to buy what we needed. What we really needed were lessons in buying groceries, as well as many other things.

Our little three-room upstairs apartment in Galena was our first home. The rent was $17.00 per month, including utilities. Each room was on a different level, but it was home to us, and we loved it for the three months we lived in it. We were in love then, and we still are these many years later. From that time forward, Eleanor has made every place we have lived a beautiful home. If it was an apartment, a parsonage, or our own home, she treated it like a mansion and decorated each beautifully. The Lord gave us such love for each other that the house was always a home.

CHAPTER 3

The Still Small Voice

Not long after we got married, I began to feel that we needed to make a move in ministry, but we didn't know anything about changing churches. We began to pray that if the Lord wanted us to move He'd open a door and send us the $100.00 we needed to pay for our wedding flowers. We never said anything to anyone else but the Lord about our desire and prayer. Shortly after this, our friends Ted and Evelyn Vibbert called.

Ted said, "Why don't you and Eleanor come with us to the Special District Council to be held in Rolla, Missouri to elect a new District Superintendent for Southern Missouri?"

I replied, "I just took this new job with the State of Missouri and can't go."

A few days later, Ted called again and said, "Bob, I feel that you guys should come and go with us."

"I'll ask my supervisor if I can take a day off to go to this meeting."

When I asked he said, "Sure, you can take it off without pay."

So, we made plans to go with the Vibberts to Rolla, Missouri—a three- or four-hour trip.

While the votes were being counted at the meeting, the Superintendent, Bert Webb, introduced various pastors, and one of them was Rev. Henry Hoar from Bethel Temple in Saint Louis. When he introduced Pastor Hoar, I turned to Eleanor and said, "That man was my parent's pastor in 1914 in Franklin, Nebraska."

After the meeting I went up to him and said, "Brother Hoar, do you remember Jesse Palmer?"

He said, "I sure do."

"I'm his youngest son."

He stepped back, looked at me, and replied, "I know Jesse, but I didn't know he had a son as young as you."

I explained that this was because my parents had two families. Leonard was 19 years older than me; Margaret, 17 years older; and Dwight, 15 years older. I went on to inform him that my parents had moved to Kansas in 1922, and two years later Paul was born, and three years later, I came on the scene. Pastor Hoar had moved away and didn't know of the two additional Palmer boys' births.

After introducing Eleanor to them and Sister Hoar to us, he asked me two important questions: "Does your wife play the piano and do you sing together?" Remember the prayer I prayed as a teenager: "I would like to have a wife who plays the piano and sings alto?" Those were the two things he asked me that day and received an answer affirmatively. God answers prayer, but that's not the end of the story.

We went and reserved a motel for the night then found a place to eat. As Ted pulled up to the Greyhound bus station in Rolla, I said, "Ted, I'm not sure I have enough money to eat here."

Eleanor spoke up and said, "Bob, you can mail that letter to your Mother in there."

I walked in the door and, to my surprise, standing just inside were Pastor Hoar, Pastor David Hastie, Eleanor's pastor, and Clyde Gunter, the Youth Director of Southern Missouri. Pastor Hoar said, "Well, here he is right now. Shall I give him the one-two?"

I didn't know what he meant, so I mailed the letter and went back outside. He followed me out and said, "How would you like to come to St. Louis and be my assistant pastor?" We spoke briefly, and he said, "I'll meet with my board on Sunday and then call you on Monday." We were so shocked by this unexpected invitation and were filled with anticipation and wonderment at what may be ahead. We later learned that Pastor Hoar had asked Pastor Hastie to take him to every motel in Rolla to find us when I just walked in. But that's not the end of the story. We stayed the night in Rolla, and returned home on Saturday.

On Sunday morning, I received the offering as usual. The morning offering was my income from the church, a very common practice of supporting a pastor in small churches. Without even looking at it, I put it in the pulpit. Following the service, after all the people left, Eleanor and I stood at the pulpit and took out the offering basket. As we looked in it, we saw 64 cents and a piece of paper. When we opened the paper we saw a check for $100.00—just what we had prayed for. We jumped into the 1935 Ford and took off for Springfield to talk with Pastor Hastie and Eleanor's parents. Pastor Hastie encouraged us to go if Pastor Hoar called us to come. Bethel Temple was one of the leading AG churches in St. Louis and of the Southern Missouri District, and we could learn so much there. We felt greatly encouraged at what was taking place in our lives.

The next day as a part of my job, I had to drive nearly to Arkansas to visit one of the people getting help from the State of Missouri. Upon my return to the office in Galena, the secretary told me I had received a long distance call from St. Louis. I told her that I would take the call at our house. When I called back, Pastor Hoar said, "We want you to come."

I said, "When?"

"Tomorrow," he replied,

I told him, "That's impossible, as I need to give notice to the office."

After a brief conversation, we decided that we should come up over Armistice Day weekend to see if we wanted to move to St. Louis and to confirm they still wanted us after meeting us. We got there and enjoyed the weekend at Bethel Temple church on Palm and Jefferson. Because Eleanor had never played an organ in church, we went to the church on Saturday and a lady showed Eleanor how to "set up" the Hammond organ. We practiced the songs I'd lead, and she did an excellent job playing on Sunday, and has been doing it for lo these

67 years. After that day, we were certain we would move to St. Louis to be the assistant pastors. Surely we can say, "He leadeth me, O blessed thought." He led us then, and still leads us today.

And God did it.

CHAPTER 4

St. Louis, Missouri, and Bethel Temple

The next few weeks were exciting as we sought someone to take our place as pastor at Galena, and to complete my work for the State. On the day after Thanksgiving in 1949, we loaded up the 1935 Ford with almost all of our possessions, including an ironing board on the running board, and moved to an apartment on the 3rd floor in the home of one of the deacons who resided several miles from the church. We lived in that apartment for a short time while an apartment next door to the church was being remodeled for us. Were we excited? You know we were. The Lord took two inexperienced 22-year-old young people and put them in the place of His choosing at the finest church in St. Louis, Missouri, to work with an experienced pastor.

We learned so much from Pastor Henry Hoar that helped

us throughout our many years of ministry. Under his guidance at Bethel Temple, we were told that at least 150 people entered full-time ministry. If a deacon or someone else wanted to preach, Pastor Hoar encouraged them to start a new church. At that time, individuals from Bethel Temple started most of the Assemblies of God churches in the St. Louis area.

What does an assistant pastor do? A simple answer could be, "Anything that needs to be done." I was the song leader, choir director, orchestra director, Christian education director, visitation leader, youth leader, bus ministry director, and preacher when needed. I loved it all. Plus, Eleanor was also very busy as organist, Sunday School teacher, junior high department superintendent, Vacation Bible School Director, and she wrote and directed Christmas programs as well as taking care of me and baby Paul, who was born a few months after we arrived. She also made draperies for all the windows in the sanctuary, plus a draw drapery for the platform. That curtain was about 40 feet wide and probably 20 feet tall, which also had a valance at the top that reached up to the ceiling. She did all of this sewing on an old-fashioned treadle sewing machine.

We were busy and happy young people. Once there at Bethel Temple we became aware that about nineteen of the young people in the church had gone to CBI, so we quickly found friends who already knew us. This was an added blessing.

And God did it.

Chapter 5

✦

Paul Eugene Palmer

One of the greatest things that happened to us was on Sunday, June 25th, 1950, when our son, Paul Eugene (named for my late brother, Paul, and Eleanor's late brother, Eugene) was born in St. Louis. The Saturday before his birth we went to the St. Louis Zoo, a great place to visit in those years. Eleanor's parents and sister Virginia had come up to see us from Springfield. We spent several hours walking around the Zoo, and then went back to our apartment.

Eleanor said, "My back hurts."

Grandma Gardner said, "We'll being having a new baby before long."

At about 9:00 p.m. on Saturday night, I took Eleanor to St. John's Hospital. After checking her in, I took her to a double door and that was the last time I saw her until after Paul was born. Things were different then from today—fathers were left outside.

After entering those doors Eleanor saw some women lying on gurneys or beds in the hall. She asked, "Have these women had their babies?"

The nurse said, "Not yet."

All seemed quiet and Eleanor thought, *Maybe this won't be too bad.*

About then she heard someone screaming in a delivery room, and she was scared, wondering what was going to happen. Back then women didn't get all the months of preparation for childbirth as they do today.

Well, I sat up all night. Eleanor's pains eased off, so she slept through the night, while I waited outside pacing back and forth and wondering what was going on. Finally, around 1:30 p.m., I was told all was well, and that I had a son. I could not have been happier with such good news. In a few minutes I went in to see Eleanor and baby Paul. What a joy that was and still is now. We are very thankful and proud of our son.

Paul was born on the very the day the Korean War began. I have told him, "There hasn't been peace on earth since you were born."

Paul was always a very smart and active little baby and young boy. He never knew a stranger, and was friendly to all and loved by all. Pastor Hoar used to carry him around the church after services. Pastor Hoar's family said he had never carried their children around like that.

Though Paul will be 67 this year, he's still that energetic person he was during his childhood and youth. I guess he was hyperactive in those days, but we didn't know it. Paul didn't want to sit still—he was always interested in something new and still is. He's a person with a great ability to relate to people old and young.

Paul has more friends and keeps in contact with more people than you can imagine. He loves to serve and was a great help to his high school band director, Mr. House, as well as to many others with whom he had contact. Paul started out playing the cornet, but Mr. House told us that he needed to transfer to baritone or tuba, as they were more needed than the cornet. It was a great change for him because he excelled on the tuba. While in high school, Paul was always very involved in Youth For Christ, and drove every week over to Kansas City, Kansas to assist the YFC Director there, even helping out when they built a large auditorium for the Youth For Christ rallies.

When he went somewhere during those years, we will always remember how he was faithful to be home on time. If we were awake when he arrived home, we heard the gravel sliding as he arrived precisely at whatever time was designated.

Paul was not an athlete, but he was the manager for one or two of the school's athletic teams. After graduating from Lee's Summit High School, Paul attended Oral Roberts University (ORU) in Tulsa, Oklahoma on a partial tuba scholarship. When Paul went to ORU, we had no money to pay the additional costs, so Eleanor applied for a job to help defray his expenses, and it was then that she began working for the IRS as a tax examiner. Paul graduated with a degree in Music Education. He is still very interested in ORU and serves on the Alumni board of directors.

One of his first jobs after graduation from college was working with TV's "The Odd Couple," Tony Randall and Jack Klugman. He was the company manager arranging their trips when they toured and performed the play by Neil Simon on which the series was based in the summers while on hiatus. Paul also worked for a firm that built a large musical auditorium center in Tulsa. He worked for the Full Gospel Business Men, as well as World Vision. While working for World Vision, he took trips to Ethiopia and India to show American businessmen what World Vision was doing in those countries. Each of these trips resulted in large sums of money being donated to World Vision.

During one such trip to Calcutta, India, he had occasion to meet Mother Teresa and was privileged to have his picture taken with her and see her ministries. Paul also met Rev. Mark Buntain, an Assemblies of God missionary, and experienced first-hand the great hospital ministry Mark and his wife, Huldah, built for the poor and needy. Paul also worked as a photographer for Crosswalk.com and Christianity.com, companies that produced church directories.

In 1983, Paul married Cheryl Ann McIntyre, and their family consists of Amy Cristine—who is single—and Michael Anthony and his wife, Mary Patricia "Trish," and their four children; Christina Alexandra, 23; Justin Michael, 20; James Christian, 14; and Joseph Michael, 10. So, we have four great-grandchildren through this union.

Paul retired in 2008 and Cheryl retired in 2016 after thirty-eight years with Kaiser Permanente, the nation's largest HMO. We are so proud of her. For the first 20+ years of her career, she was an OB-GYN nurse practitioner; the final nine years she was the administrator for the Pediatrics Department at the Kaiser facility in Riverside, California. The department had a staff of more than 50 doctors and 80 nurses, plus other support personnel.

Paul and Cheryl are quite happy enjoying their motorhome and newfound freedom from day-to-day work. They all live in Corona, California. We are very thankful for this great part of our family.

CHAPTER 6

Sundays at Bethel

Classes were held for all ages and interests. In fact, in the main auditorium we had a class for men on the platform, a singles youth class and two ladies' classes and a young marrieds class on the main floor, plus another in the balcony. The basement had two small auditoriums with classrooms all around for children. Additional classes for the youth were held next door in three apartments. We had Sunday School contests and loyalty contests and gave out banners, etc. The church was alive and doing well. Attendance for all teachers and leaders was mandated—you had to be faithful if you were going to be a teacher. I think that one Sunday we had 581 present for Sunday School. We had three buses that traveled all over the north part of St. Louis bringing in children, so that they could learn about Jesus. Only eternity will reveal how many lives were changed through the efforts of the many men and women and young people who taught and helped in those classes. Serving God was, and is, the most important thing we could do. Most of the bus-ministry children received personal home visits from their teachers or bus drivers weekly or regularly.

And we had church.

Worshipers filled the auditorium on Sunday mornings, and Sunday nights saw the auditorium well-filled, too. At each service there was an altar call for everyone. The gifts of the Spirit were in evidence as people were filled with the Holy Spirit. Revival meetings were conducted regularly. Shortly before we went to Bethel an evangelist, Oral Roberts preached one day. This was just as his ministry started to be known nationwide. On Sunday nights people came out and there was great singing and great preaching by Pastor Hoar and, sometimes, others. We were so blessed to be a part of that great church. One of the best things about Bethel Temple was the atmosphere— God was there. His Presence cannot be manufactured—only God can move as He did.

We spent four wonderful years with Pastor and Mrs. Hoar and the Bethel congregation, and learned so much about the moving of the Holy Spirit. We saw souls saved, and people entered the ministry in the local church and in other places. We still have friends from those four years. We were extremely busy, but we loved the work of the Lord. At Bethel, we really began to develop our ministries. By the time we left there, I preached many Sunday and Wednesday nights. God had used us to help the congregation to grow both in numbers and spiritually. It was a great time of growth for us working in a good strong church, and especially with Pastor Henry Hoar.

And God did it.

CHAPTER 7

✦

Evangelism Beckons

After four years at Bethel we felt that we should make a move, so we scheduled three revival meetings with friends and launched forth as evangelists right after Thanksgiving in 1953. We quickly learned that just before Christmas was not a wise time to be evangelists as most churches were busy with Christmas events.

Thank the Lord for Eleanor's parents who let us leave some of our belongings with them. We owned only one piece of furniture—a small cabinet-style record player. As we began our Evangelistic Ministry, we traveled from St. Louis to Springfield, then on to Arkansas, Michigan, and Missouri—preaching almost every night. In those days, Eleanor and I sang together, and she accompanied us on the accordion. It was while these meetings were being conducted that we heard the

Rev. C.M. Ward, speaker on "Revivaltime," the national radio broadcast of the Assemblies of God. Rev. Ward informed the audience that the state of North Carolina had only 40 Assemblies of God churches. In Missouri it seemed that almost every town, at least around Springfield, had an AG Church.

After hearing C.M. Ward say there was a great need in North Carolina to start more churches, I received a burden for North Carolina.

I decided to write to the Superintendent, Andrew Stirling and offer to come and start a church. My letter was somewhat like a resume, though at the time I didn't know what a resume was. The letter detailed what we'd done. He immediately wrote back and offered to get me two weekend meetings, so we could come to North Carolina and pick a city where we wanted to start a church.

After a while, when I didn't hear from him, I contacted him by phone. He told me that one pastor had resigned and another one became ill, so they couldn't have us. I thought, *I guess it is not God's will for us at this time to go to North Carolina.* But as the days went by, I still felt a burden and interest in going there.

In the meantime, we conducted a revival meeting in a town not too far away in Buffalo, Missouri. The church was a nice building and a fair group of people gathered in it night after night. However, the pastor and his wife lived in an uncompleted house, and we stayed there with them. One night after the sermon, a young woman came to the altar when most of the people had already left to go home. Those of us who stayed were blessed to see her filled with the Holy Spirit. We learned later that she became a student at Central Bible Institute. The meeting came to a close, and for the three-week meeting we received a total of $51.00 in offerings. Oh, did I mention that between the church and the parsonage was a huge hole in the road? So we had to walk a block or so to get across the street. But we loved the work of the Lord anyway.

And God did it.

The next day we returned to Springfield, and I went to the Southern Missouri District office to pay my tithes. The Assistant Superintendent, Rev. V.L. Hertweck saw me and said, "Bob, where is your next revival meeting?"

I replied, "In Butler, Missouri."

He said, "Oh, you know the Pastor has resigned and moved away?"

I replied, "No, I sent him my promotional materials and he didn't write or call me." It was quite disturbing to learn that one's next meeting was cancelled without any message in advance.

Reverend Hertweck said, "Don't worry, Bob, come tomorrow, and we'll go to a fellowship meeting. I'll help you get another engagement."

So, Eleanor and I went with him to the meeting, but no one seemed interested in us. "Don't worry," he said, "tomorrow we'll go to another meeting in the western part near Kansas."

When we arrived, we were delighted to learn that a former classmate from CBI was there. He came up to me and said, "I've been wanting to schedule you for a revival. When can you start?"

I said, "How about tomorrow night?"

He said, "Let's make it next Sunday night." So, our need for another meeting was quickly settled. Since we were in Springfield, we decided to attend church on Sunday morning at Calvary Temple, formerly Southside AG, where Jack West was the pastor. That morning Pastor West informed the congregation that Bob and Eleanor Palmer were from their church and were there today as traveling evangelists. He went on to state that the people needed to help us as we went from church to church. And so it was with those words that Pastor West took up a love offering which gave us $200.00. So, you see, the Lord does know how to supply our needs as we trust and serve Him.

And God did it.

That Sunday night we began a revival ministry at First Assembly of God in El Dorado Springs, Missouri. I don't remember too much about the church, except that it was while there I still felt a burden for North Carolina. We continued praying as to what the Lord would have us to do. I looked at encyclopedias and maps, and at last I wrote another letter to Andrew Stirling, stating that if he could get me even one weekend, we'd come. At that time gasoline was about 15 cents a gallon, so it was not too expensive to make a trip like that. He received my letter a few days later and that same night met with the church board in Dunn, North Carolina.

At the meeting, the board wondered if any other pastors in North Carolina would be interested in coming to Dunn. After some discussion, one of them said, "Brother Stirling, do you know anyone even in Springfield that might be interested in coming here?"

He replied, "As a matter of fact, there is a young man there who seems determined that God wants him to come to North Carolina. I just received a letter from him today. I have his original letter in my briefcase that tells a little about him and his wife." He read my first letter to them, and one of the members said, "He sounds like he'd be a good man for here. Do you know how to contact him?" My second letter had told him that I was in El Dorado Springs, Missouri for a revival meeting.

That night, Andrew Stirling called the Assembly of God parsonage number in El Dorado, and the pastor said that the call was for me. God be praised that small church had listed a parsonage phone. When I answered the phone, I was surprised it was Andrew Stirling.

He asked, "Would you be interested in an existing church?"

I asked, "What kind of a church is it?"

"Frankly, brother, it is the largest Assembly in the North Carolina District," he replied.

I hadn't asked for an existing church, but God in His wisdom and knowledge allowed us to be considered for it.

Five weeks later, we were candidates for and elected as the pastors. God does lead and guide His children. I was twenty-seven years old when I became the pastor of Glad Tidings church. When we arrived on April 18, 1954, for our first real pastorate, the church had an average attendance of 250.

And God did it.

Chapter 8

✥

Dunn, North Carolina, and Glad Tidings Assembly of God

We loved it in North Carolina. We all need to remember, however, that just because we're in God's will does not mean we won't have any problems. In fact, the devil doesn't like it when God has His way, so Satan tries to disrupt what God is doing. I had a lot to learn and, fortunately, the Lord allowed us to learn. We spent five years in Dunn at Glad Tidings Assembly of God, and God blessed our ministry with many people giving their lives to Christ. Others were filled with the Holy Spirit, the attendance grew, and we started a daily radio broadcast during a revival meeting with Rev. G.L. Johnson, who later served for 40 years as pastor of the Peoples Church in Fresno, California. For some of the five years we were in Dunn, the "Revival Hour" was on the air.

During our time as pastors in Dunn, two floors were added

to the church's education building. This provided much needed classroom space for the Sunday School. We enjoyed the beautiful state of North Carolina with its gracious people, the Atlantic Ocean, and the mountains. While living there, I learned to eat fish—red snapper was my favorite—and we went to the ocean several times. However, I was afflicted with seasickness, so our daughter Phyllis and I looked for seashells, while Eleanor, Paul, and our friends the Burnetts, fished.

Since 1959, we have returned and spoken three or four times at the Glad Tidings church. A new church was built in a new location, and a window and pew were put in the building in our honor. We were invited to be there for the dedication.

One year while pastoring in Dunn, I also led the District Youth Conference in the mountains at the AG Campground in Cullasaja near Franklin, south of Asheville. During our latest trip to Dunn in August 2015, I was given the opportunity to preach the Word and sing. There were at least fourteen people present who'd been in the congregation when we left in April 1959. It was good to visit once again and to be in the place where we learned so much in our youth.

CHAPTER 9

✧

Phyllis Elaine Palmer Comstock

The most important personal thing that happened in Dunn was the birth of our lovely daughter, Phyllis Elaine, on December 17, 1955. Phyllis has added so much blessing to us throughout the years with her love and beauty. She was a little "Tar Heel" with a great southern accent for the first few years of her life. We lived in Dunn until she was three-and-a-half years old.

Ours was a very busy street, so we tried to keep a close watch on her. However, one day a neighbor called and said that Phyllis was on top of a house about two houses away. Many of the homes in that area were flat roofed. She had found a way to climb on top of a fifty-gallon barrel and got on the roof.

At Glad Tidings, Phyllis sat on the front row as Eleanor played the organ. She was always good in school and was a perfect example of a Christian young person wherever she lived. Phyllis played the flute in the school band in junior high and high school. She has always loved to sing and has performed many solos as well as singing in the music worship team in churches.

During a revival meeting with Charles and Frances Hunter in Ottumwa, Iowa, where we lived and pastored at the time, Phyllis, who's spiritually sensitive, was greatly blessed by the Lord in that meeting and by a message from ORU's musical group, Living Sound. The anointing she received that evening inspired her decision to attend Bethany Bible College in Scott's Valley, California, to prepare for the work of the Lord. Her Grandmother, Hattie Palmer, and Aunt, Margaret Bond lived in the area along with several other Palmer family members. At Bethany, she played the flute in a recording made by the college orchestra led by Noel Wilson. It's wonderful how God works as Phyllis had originally made plans to follow in her brother's footsteps and attend ORU.

I remember so well the morning we prepared to drive from Ottumwa to Minneapolis to board a plane to California. As I shaved, I heard crying in the kitchen and went to see just what was going on. I found Phyllis and Eleanor crying as Phyllis said, "I'm too young to leave home." Nevertheless, we made the trip and she adjusted to California very well, especially after she met Rick Comstock.

Nearly a year later in August, it was not "back to school" but, instead, Phyllis and Rick were married in a lovely ceremony that took place on the campus in the chapel. During the year after their marriage, they became youth pastors for a Presbyterian church in the Santa Cruz area while Rick finished his schooling. After Rick graduated from Bethany Bible College, they received a call to Arroyo Grande, California. During their ten years of ministry at Arroyo Grande, they served as youth pastor, associate pastor, and interim pastor. After that they were elected as pastors in Atascadero, California.

We are so blessed that Phyllis and Rick have been in the ministry all of their forty-one years of married life in Arroyo Grande and Atascadero. Phyllis has lived her life as the wife of a minister. Since 1975, Phyllis and Rick have blessed so many people, young and old. Their two sons, Christopher and Casey, have blessed us, too. Chris and Casey both graduated from high school and Cal Poly while living in Atascadero.

Casey and his wife Theresa (nee Broussard from Beaumont, Texas) have brought two beautiful babies into our lives as well (Lily Kate, five years old, and Maddy Beth, three years old). On March 20, 2016, Chris married the lovely Catalina Padilla, who hails from Costa Rica. On August 28, 2016, Rick and Phyllis retired from pastoral service after twenty-nine years pastoring First Assembly of God in Atascadero. That's quite a record. We are so proud of all of them.

Phyllis worked as a secretary for the Atascadero Unified School District for more than 28 years. In 2011, she was featured in an article on the front page of the local newspaper as the Outstanding Classified Employee for her work in the School District and for the life she lived among them. Phyllis and Rick still live in their home they built near the church in Atascadero. We have enjoyed being close to both of our children and their families during the past 37 years in Southern California.

CHAPTER 10

⬩

Leaving Dunn

The ministers and delegates of the North Carolina District elected me to serve on the General Presbytery of the Assemblies of God. Three Ministers from each district were selected to serve in this capacity. This was a great privilege and honor to serve in this way. At the same time, my brother, Leonard Palmer served on the General Presbytery from Northern California. As General Presbyter I was also on the board of Southeastern Bible College, now Southeastern University, in Lakeland, Florida. This, too, was an honor and privilege, and we got to travel to Florida for a board meeting and to a general Presbyters meeting in Springfield, Missouri. That was great as we were also able to visit Eleanor's family.

After five years of fruitful ministry in Dunn, Eleanor and I both felt that it was time to resign and become evangelists again. As I mentioned previously, sometimes when a pastor felt it was time to go to another location or ministry, he'd call some friends and schedule three revival meetings. So, this is what we did, again trusting God to lead us into whatever ministry He had planned for us.

It was not easy to leave Dunn. We made so many wonderful friends during the years. A great group of people were in the church. Many tears were shed at the last service we conducted. We will never forget those people who gave us love and support while we were young pastors. We have great memories of living in the "Tar Heel" state, and still have many friends there today. We look back on those days realizing that some great things were accomplished only through Him.

And God did it.

CHAPTER 11

On the Road Again

We packed up our furniture and the things that we didn't need while traveling and stored them at the home of a couple from the church. On April 18, 1959, we headed for Springfield, Missouri to Eleanor's parents' home which was our address while we traveled. We greatly appreciated their hospitality and that of her sister, Virginia. Paul still had a little more school to finish, so he stayed with Grandma and Grandpa Gardner and Aunt Virginia for several weeks as we went to our first revival meeting in Arkansas. We had quite a schedule: Arkansas, Michigan, Pennsylvania, and Roanoke, Virginia, where I was a candidate for the church. We preached for three nights, but did not feel like it was where God wanted us. So, I talked to their board and told them we didn't feel that Roanoke was where we were led to be.

The next day, we packed the car and returned to Missouri. We enjoyed the few months in evangelistic ministry, but we were, and are, pastors. Eleanor and I had confidence the Lord would guide us into His perfect will for our family's future. And, as this story proceeds, you will find that He did guide us—time and time again.

When we arrived in Missouri it was camp meeting time at the Lake of the Ozarks, so we went for a day. No sooner had we arrived when friends told us about the church in Lee's Summit, Missouri, and how it needed a pastor. They were in a building program, and the church had been without a pastor for several weeks. Their pastor had accepted a call to another church in Sikeston, Missouri. Five or six different candidates preached, but to no avail. One withdrew his name, and the others didn't receive sufficient votes to be elected as pastor. We made contact with the church, but another candidate was already scheduled for the following Sunday.

The next week we went back to the Lake, and the Presbyter was there. He told us that the candidate had not been elected, and another candidate was already scheduled for the next Sunday. So, I scheduled a revival to start the following Sunday in Cape Girardeau, Missouri, because I felt that the person would be elected. However, on the Wednesday night following his preaching, he was not elected.

The Presbyter said the church wanted us to come the next Sunday. I called the pastor and asked if we could start the revival meeting on Monday night instead of Sunday. After kidding me a little he agreed. He had two sons in the ministry and understood how important it was to be available when a church set a date for a candidate to preach, and become pastor if elected.

That Saturday, Eleanor and I drove up to Lee's Summit to meet the official board, to prepare for Sunday, and to meet the congregation at First Assembly of God. As we drove along Highway 71 and made a right turn onto Highway 50, we realized we were entering a new town and a new challenge from the Lord. As we drove under the railroad bridge we had our first glimpse of the church building. There before our eyes was a small restaurant, a filling station, and an unfinished church building right next door to the Lee's Summit High School. Almost instantly I saw the building finished. The opportunity to be involved in that task was a formidable challenge.

On Sunday morning I preached, we sang, and we saw someone come to the altar to be saved. Eleanor and I met the board that afternoon, and then conducted another service in the evening. Both services were blessed by the Lord. We then headed back to Springfield for the night. The business meeting was the next Wednesday night, so we waited a few days to learn the congregation's decision. The next day, we headed to Cape Girardeau for the previously scheduled revival to commence that night.

We lived in expectation of what would happen in Lee's Summit when the business meeting was held on Wednesday. I had told the pastor that we'd stay there in Cape Girardeau two weeks, regardless of what the decision was in Lee's Summit. Following the revival service on Wednesday night, we received a call from the Presbyter in Lee's Summit informing us of the favorable vote. We rejoiced in the outcome, and immediately began praying and planning for the days ahead.

We spent two weeks in the revival, as well as helping Pastor Shoults lay the footings for a new addition to the building. It was here that Paul had fun staying in the small "teardrop" house trailer belonging to the pastor. One night while Eleanor and I sang, Phyllis decided to play on the piano. Lots of fun things happened while traveling as evangelists with two children.

We finished a successful revival meeting in Cape Girardeau and headed back to Springfield to pack and move to our new church in Lee's Summit. Next door to the old church, a parsonage was for sale to make some cash available for the new building. We'd live in the parsonage temporarily and purchase our own home soon.

And God did it.

CHAPTER 12

⬦

Lee's Summit, Missouri,
and First Assembly of God

The next day we drove from Springfield to Lee's Summit to meet and to become acquainted with the people of the First Assembly of God church. We drove into town and again saw a view of the unfinished church building, which looked like an abandoned project. There were no windows, and it was exposed to the rain, dust, birds, and mice. In my mind's eye, I saw a completed church. God gave us the vision for the job, and the people voted to elect us to lead them.

As soon as we arrived, Ray Reed, Secretary of the church board and I rented a U-Haul-type truck and left for North Carolina for the move to Missouri. We drove nonstop to Dunn, loaded the truck, and drove back to Lee's Summit without sleeping. We drove approximately 1,800 miles. Yes, we were tired, but I had to preach my first sermon as pastor upon arriving back in Lee's Summit. The title of the sermon was "Expectations: What You Can Expect from Me What We Can Expect from You—What We All Can Expect from God."

Within a few weeks of arrival, the parsonage was sold to the Nazarene church and we purchased a brand new three-bedroom house for only $14,250.00. Only 884 square feet, it was a small house with a basement and a single garage. We loved having our own place. We finished the basement making a family room and an additional bedroom and half bath for Paul. After we moved to Ottumwa, Iowa and later Hawthorne, California, we kept the house as a rental. Eventually, we sold it for a profit after renting it for about 10 years.

Our family had come to a place where we would spend more than eleven happy years. Some of the most productive years of our lives were the years we lived in Lee's Summit. Paul graduated from Lee's Summit High School, and Phyllis was there until midway through 9th grade. Our children had it all: Great public schools to attend; good friends in and out of the church; agreeable youth camps to go to at the Lake of the Ozarks; and a wonderful church to attend.

When we arrived in Lee's Summit, the church building was only one-third finished without the necessary funds to complete it. My main task was to lead the people to finish the building. Every Sunday after the regular tithes and offering were received, I would lay my open Bible on the communion table and we had a march to bring in an offering for the building fund. We had this march every Sunday—even after we moved upstairs from the basement—until the sanctuary was completed. For about 18 months the church met in the lower floor with mice running around, whitewash paint chips falling down from the ceiling, uncomfortable metal chairs to sit on, no nursery, and no enclosed classrooms. Even water ran across the floor when it rained. We also had to build many other necessities, such as attendance, financial stability, and spiritual growth, and develop all the characteristics that a church must have in order to be successful to reach into the community. It was not an easy task, but we loved every minute of it.

Of course, we experienced some difficult times. The bank that loaned the church $25,000.00 said they would not loan any more money. At that time, the Minister's Benefit Association of the Assemblies of God was in its early days of church financing, and money was not available through them either. However, I found out that Pastor Herschel Barnett, father of Rev. Tommy Barnett from Kansas City, Kansas, was on the board of a bank in Kansas City, Kansas. I went to see him and, through his influence, we were able to obtain a small additional loan from the bank, providing the building was enclosed.

I then asked the congregation if anyone could loan us the money so we could buy the necessary materials to get the church airtight and watertight. That morning two different couples offered to do just that. One couple had the money available immediately, so we borrowed it and began to enclose the building. Another man, a carpenter named Carl West, dedicated an entire month to getting the windows in place. (Later, I was told that because of Carl's giving that month to the church, he was never out of work again while he was a full-time carpenter.)

On the day it began snowing, we installed the last window in the balcony. The church was airtight and watertight as requested by the bank. Because of this, the money became available to pay for the windows and doors, and to pay back the loan to that faithful couple who advanced the money to the church.

Little by little, the building was finished. As the years passed by, I developed more and more appreciation for the people of God who helped us pastors get the job done. We can't do it alone—it is God's work and all can help. We are all "laborers together with God." What an honor and privilege to be a part of God's work.

From the time we arrived, I worked the day shift mixing cement for the one hired bricklayer, carrying bricks, and building scaffolding. Then in the evenings I worked the second shift, as men, women and young people came to help do what they could do. The people had a mind to work, and routinely said things along the lines of, "We're glad to help. We only ask that what we need is on hand when we get here." That is what we did.

By Easter of 1960, we moved upstairs into the yet uncarpeted sanctuary. We still sat in metal chairs, and the platform contained the faded green carpet that was on the floor in the basement where we previously conducted services. But it was a victorious day when we moved upstairs. The people invested in the building because they gave their money, sacrificed their time, bent their backs, used their abilities, and contributed their efforts to see the new church emerge.

Many of the people came night after night to help with the completion of the interior, such as laying the floor tile, putting up mahogany plywood around the platform, sanding and cleaning the laminated beams, and washing the wood ceiling with a Clorox solution to get rid of the mildew that had spawned. The hot water furnace was in, and men put in the heat radiators upstairs. After we arrived, the only other paid labor was for the plastering of the interior walls, the tower outside, and the laying of the carpet. Volunteers did all the rest of the work, inside and out.

On the first Sunday service held upstairs, a fine couple, A.J. and Mary McCoy came forward to accept Christ. They were the first of many who would come to know the Lord during the next eleven years, and they became active, faithful members. The McCoys had two girls about the same ages as Phyllis and Paul, and we all became close friends. A.J. became the youth leader and, eventually, one of the deacons. He was also the lead painter at a factory that manufactured those "cherry pickers" seen around most construction sites and along the roads where telephone and electric lines were installed or repaired. The company was building a new paint shop and, as the lead painter, A.J. was expecting to get the foreman's position. When the building was done, the job was given to another man.

Naturally, A.J. was greatly disappointed, and as a new Christian, he was really discouraged. A.J. came to me and said, "I was better off before I got saved and began tithing." He was ready to quit his job and try to find another.

I said, "Don't quit this job until you have a new one." Then I said, "A.J., you are a qualified painter, why don't you put an ad in the paper to paint houses during the summer days? That will give you some more money."

He listened and took my advice. A.J. only got one job from a lady who called him who also happened to be a Christian. He painted her house.

Before A.J. finished painting the house, his boss called him in and said, "We should have given you the foreman's job to begin with. The guy who became the foreman painter messed things up. We need you to run the automatic paint shop."

A.J. was promoted, received a raise, and from then on was used by the company in several different positions until he finally became the plant manager. The lesson is: "Honor God, work hard, and God will bless you in every way. You may have trials along the way, but remain faithful."

When we moved from the basement to the upstairs auditorium you couldn't imagine the difference in the atmosphere of the church. After being down in the dark for so long, it was so light upstairs. However, it was the Spirit of the Lord who really brought the light into the church. The balcony was not yet finished, nor was the carpet laid, but we finished those things rather quickly—by comparison to the other elements that were necessary to accomplish in eight or nine months of hard work.

During that first year in Lee's Summit, I learned so much about building and raising money. We had a wonderful congregation there, and the people were so good to us and to Paul and Phyllis. We have often remarked about that group of people who were there when we arrived in 1959. I think Paul and Phyllis have had good attitudes about church because of those members in that church. We heard how some church people subjected ministers' children to severe criticism, but Lee's Summit was a great place to raise our children.

And God did it.

As the church grew, it became evident that we needed to expand and build more classrooms, so we began planning to add a two-story addition to the present building. This included a small chapel, nursery, half-sized gym, restrooms on the first floor, and several more classrooms on the second floor. The expansion blended in well with our present building and was a great addition. This building was built by a local contractor, and as such, was a great relief to me and to all the others who had worked so hard in finishing the sanctuary. The contractor said it was one of the smoothest jobs he'd done—particularly because he received all of his payments quickly.

By planning ahead, we showed the congregation that we could make the payments from the regular tithes and offerings. Therefore, we didn't require any fund-raising programs. By building a strong financial foundation, a credit union loaned all the necessary funds to complete the new structure. In addition, we had saved enough money, proving to the congregation, as well as any lender, our ability to take care of the payments.

Without a doubt, Lee's Summit, Missouri was an ideal place for us to pastor. The church was stable. It had enough people to sustain itself, had great confidence in our leadership and in the official board. A cooperative congregation, they were willing to work together with their pastor. We had, and still have friends at Lee's Summit, even though we've been gone for more than 47 years.

Many people, both young and old, were saved during the

years we were in Lee's Summit. One of the great conversions that took place was that of Laura Nulik. She was raised in an Assemblies of God church in Oklahoma. From the age of 9 she played the piano in church. Greatly talented, Laura felt the call of the world, and departed from the Lord to became a pianist in nightclubs "where the lights were turned down low." She wandered for many years until the day she drove by the church and saw the cross on the tower. Laura said to her husband Tom; "I'm going there to church next Sunday."

We were in the midst of a revival meeting with Evangelist Jack Reddick. When he preached, people got saved. Jack "laid everything on the table," and that morning Laura came home to God. She was a transformed woman from then on. Immediately, the Lord gave her beautiful songs, and she sang them in church. The first song that the Lord gave to Laura was, "Every Time I Pass A Church." When she sang that song, there was an immediate response and people came to the altars. There was no preaching. The words were so anointed. About a year later, Laura's husband, Tom called me. We met, and he also gave his heart and life to Christ.

These questions come to me from an old song:

> *How many are the lost that I have lifted?*
> *How many are the chained I've helped to free?*

What a challenge to each of us. Thank God for such a great Savior who still brings the wanderers home. Just listening to Laura's voice on compact disc more than 50 years later still brings tears to our eyes.

After about ten years in Lee's Summit we began to sense that our work there might be finished, and that the Lord was leading us to consider other places in which to pastor. In fact, we had two definite invitations to go elsewhere, one in Tennessee and one in Arizona. We went and preached, but we felt neither place was God's will for us. So we were not disappointed when we were not confirmed as pastor at either church. It is not always easy to discern the will of God, and it requires some patience on our part.

In the fall of 1970, we made a trip to Israel. While there, I told the Lord, "I will stay in Lee's Summit the rest of my life unless you open the door without my having to do anything. I will not be applying for any more churches. So, when you want us to move, it will be up to you to cause it to happen without my doing anything. Thy will be done in our lives as you will it."

We returned from our trip to Israel on a Friday. On Saturday morning, I went to the church as usual to finish preparing for the Sunday services. A young man from the church was sitting in my office when the phone rang. It was a long-distance call, and I asked him to step outside so I could speak in private with whoever was calling.

The voice on the phone said, "This is Rex Moore from First Pentecostal Assembly of God in Ottumwa, Iowa. Where have you been? I've been trying to call you for a couple of weeks."

"We've been on a trip to Israel and just returned last night," I replied.

He said, "I'm chairman of the board up here, and you've been recommended as a possible candidate to be our pastor."

"Who recommended us?"

"Rev. T. E. Gannon, Assistant General Superintendent of the Assemblies of God."

I was greatly surprised because I knew Rev. Gannon by reputation, but had never ever talked with him about anything. He had also been the Superintendent of the Iowa District in the past, so he knew the church in Ottumwa quite well. Several months later we met up at the Iowa District Council in Des Moines.

Rev. Gannon said, "I guess you were surprised at my recommending you."

"Yes, I was. How did you decide to do that?"

"We keep our eyes open."

The lesson we learned from this experience is that we never know who's watching us, and our actions or lack of actions which may very well result in positive or negative results to us.

To make a long story shorter, Eleanor, Phyllis and I made the decision to take a trip up to Ottumwa. For some time, Eleanor and I felt restless in our spirits. This prospect came about only after my earnest prayer to the Lord while in Israel. We could not fail to respond by at least exploring the possibility.

We arrived in Ottumwa to meet and be interviewed by the board. After seeing the beautiful church building and town, we instinctively felt that we should accept the opportunity to preach and to be candidates for the pastorate. I called a board meeting in Lee's Summit to inform the official board that we'd received an unsolicited call from First Pentecostal Assembly of God in Ottumwa, Iowa and would go up there in a couple of weeks to preach, to meet the congregation, and to be voted on as pastors.

I think it was at that time that one of the board members said, "If you are considering leaving, perhaps we should start looking for a new pastor."

I realized right then that if we weren't elected, we needed to go ahead and leave. Fortunately, we didn't have to leave on those terms, as the First Pentecostal Assembly of God in Ottumwa elected us as their pastors.

Thus, we made a life-changing decision about our future and our ministry in Lee's Summit. We finished on the last Sunday of December 1970. It was not easy to break the ties of more than 11 years. Later we found out how hard it was for Phyllis to leave her friends—both in and out of the Lee's Summit Church and Lee's Summit Junior High School. We had been blessed by the church's cooperation in everything throughout those years, but it "was God calling" and we must obey.

And God did it.

CHAPTER 13

✧

Ottumwa, Iowa, and First Pentecostal Assembly of God

We began our new ministry on the first Sunday of January 1971 at the First Pentecostal Assembly of God in Ottumwa, Iowa. A snowstorm with heavy, wet snow surprised most of the residents. There were only 54 in Sunday School and 56 in church that morning. No Sunday night service was even attempted. The next Sunday, we had attendance of 200 to 250.

The church was a beautiful, yellow brick building with a sanctuary seating 700 people. It had a fully carpeted basement, and a balcony that reached up to the beams at the back of the auditorium. It was the most beautiful church in town right on Church Street. It spoke well of the vision of the board and former pastor, John Walker, who worked long and hard to see the church to completion before he had accepted an invitation to a large church in Nebraska.

Ottumwa, Iowa, was an old river town on the Des Moines River in Wapello County. The river ran right through the center of the city dividing it in two. Most of the business area and more expensive homes were on the north side of the river, but First Pentecostal Assembly of God was one of the leading churches in the city in the main business area on the south side of the river. The church had been in the same part of the city since the days of the Great Depression and was noted for the thousands of people who were fed from its doors during those difficult days. A strong and vibrant church, it had only five pastors in 50 years, so it had quite a history. We were the fifth.

Upon our arrival, we moved into the parsonage of the church where we resided for the four-and-a-half years we ministered there. It was an adequate house, but not like having our own home. The basement was fixed up as a meeting place for the women's missionary group which had met there during the sojourn of previous pastors.

The wife of one of the deacons told us of the arrangement, but quickly offered, "It is up to you. If you would prefer not to have meetings in your home, you don't have to continue it."

They also made use of the refrigerator in the kitchen during those meetings. She said to anyone who mentioned the change, "How would you like having a group meeting in your basement regularly?"

The accommodation was made, and no problems arose because of it. As a result, in just a little more than a year, the new fellowship hall was planned and soon under construction next door to the church. A covered walkway joined the church and fellowship hall.

Shortly after coming to Ottumwa, we decided to attend the "Pastor's School" in Hammond, Indiana, at the great First Baptist Church where Jack Hyles was the pastor. It was a tremendous blessing to go there. Our vision was revitalized, and we received great foresight for what could be done for God in Ottumwa.

We returned with new vigor and vitality for the Lord. The church already had a Sunday radio ministry which was soon expanded to be a seven-day per week radio ministry on a local station. We first had a 15-minute daily broadcast, but this later was reduced to five minutes daily. I often took a regular Sunday or Wednesday night sermon and divided it into five sections for a part each day. It was called "The Pastor's Call." This broadcast continued as long as we were the Pastors in Ottumwa. Because of this, I often spoke as many as seven or eight times per week, though some were short sermons on the air. We were very busy in Ottumwa.

We started a bus ministry with four buses and two vans which brought many children to Sunday School and church. There was a constant spirit of revival in the church, and for one six-month period there was a water baptismal service held each week but one. God was glorified in the services, and many new people became a part of First Pentecostal Assembly of God.

After two or three years, we led the congregation to build the much-needed large fellowship hall. One of the older men, a retired builder, was in charge and did a wonderful job. He and I did much of the layout of the building and preparation for the foundation and floor to be poured. Premade trusses were used, and he insisted they be strengthened before allow-ing them to be put in place. The fellowship hall was connected to the main church with a covered walkway so that people could get into the church or fellowship hall without getting wet.

This building became one of the most used areas of the church. It had a very good kitchen, plus a large room where an intern or guest could stay, in addition to the larger area. The main room measured 42 feet by 96 feet in size. Our adult Sunday class filled the large space and, eventually, the space could be divided into smaller rooms by folding partitions for more classes. It became a meeting place for men who came to play table tennis, as well as a place for youth meetings and teachers meetings. Recently, it was expanded through the purchase of a nearby building. The church complex is beautiful.

During the building of the fellowship hall, I ruptured a disk in my neck and had to have surgery. I went to a local doctor who referred me to a surgeon in Des Moines. After arriving at his office, we discovered he was a "lower back" surgeon. Another doctor's name was offered, but a lady in the church who was an anesthesiologist said, "Let me check this doctor out." After talking to some nurses she knew in Des Moines, they suggested that it was better for me to go to Kansas City. She called a surgeon in Kansas City who she knew and made an appointment for me. Thank God she was acquainted with a good surgeon in Kansas City. There was no room available that week, so I returned a week later for the surgery. I had my surgery there in 1972 and have had no further problems.

While I was hospitalized in Kansas City, I was put into a room with a man who told his wife, "Don't bring any of those

%#@! preachers to see me," and I just happened to be put in the room with him. The Lord doesn't give up.

We had some very good conversations while we were both patients. He told me he had a praying mother and, while she was alive, he had many accidents, but was never injured seriously until after she had died.

I never saw him after he went home from the hospital, but I sincerely hope that our conversations resulted in his coming to Christ.

It's amazing the ways the Lord can lead us into situations like this one where we can witness for Him. While I was hospitalized, some of the Lee's Summit church contingency came to see us. Eleanor stayed with friends. When I was cleared for travel the Nuliks drove us back to Ottumwa. The Lord has His people everywhere willing to bless those of us who are in the ministry. Thank God for His people in every church.

And God did it.

We really enjoyed our four-and-a-half years in Ottumwa, as we were the recipients of many blessings from the Lord while pastoring there. One outstanding meeting conducted in Ottumwa was with the "Happy Hunters." Charles and Francis Hunter came for a short meeting during which many people were blessed. Their message of "Divine Healing: Baptism with the Holy Spirit and Deliverance From Smoking" was well received. One night, 55 ministers from various churches in the area attended the meeting. It richly blessed us, and the church people were encouraged as hundreds gathered in day services at the church and many more at night in the Armory. People came from several churches in the community. Some were healed of various diseases, and others were delivered from smoking. Several were filled with the Holy Spirit. A real moving of God came in those few days. Churches today need that kind of moving of God's Spirit.

And God did it.

Many Pentecostal churches were in Ottumwa, but First Pentecostal was the largest Spirit-filled church. There was a real spirit of revival and cooperation among the various churches in town. Several non-Pentecostal ministers gathered together in regular prayer meetings, and God richly blessed them. Eleanor and I team-taught a married couples class that sometimes had 100 in the class—of all ages. During the years we were in Ottumwa, we experienced great support from the congregation and the official board.

We had heard upon arriving in Ottumwa that First Pentecostal Assembly of God was always in "A revival or a revolution." While we were pastors we're thankful it was in a time of revival. It's not always easy to be a pastor, especially of an "older congregation" who has its mind made up as to how things should or should not be done. However, the Lord gave us wisdom and respect from the congregation, and we had a minimum of problems while we ministered there. We've enjoyed going back and preaching several times since 1975, after relocating to Southern California.

It was and still is a great church in Ottumwa. A few years

ago, we asked our grandson, Chris Comstock, to accompany us on a return trip so that he could see and meet the great people there. We've been so blessed of God to be pastors from the Midwest, East, and West during our years of ministry. We went to each place in God's will—and believe that we left at God's time.

When Rex Moore, one of the board members in Ottumwa, discovered that Eleanor had worked for the IRS, he hired her to work in his office, which included tax preparation. As she typed 900 income tax returns each year from an adding machine tape, it was a great learning experience for her while she worked there. Rex also did insurance and real estate, and he was the church treasurer, so Eleanor learned bookkeeping from him as well. She was, and is, a multi-talented person. How blessed I am that the Lord brought our lives together nearly two years after I had graduated from Central Bible Institute.

And God did it.

above: Eleanor, Paul, and Robert,
St. Louis, MO, c. 1953;
right: Bethel Temple, St. Louis, MO;
below: Bus ministry was big at Bethel Temple.
Paul is seen standing behind the fence.

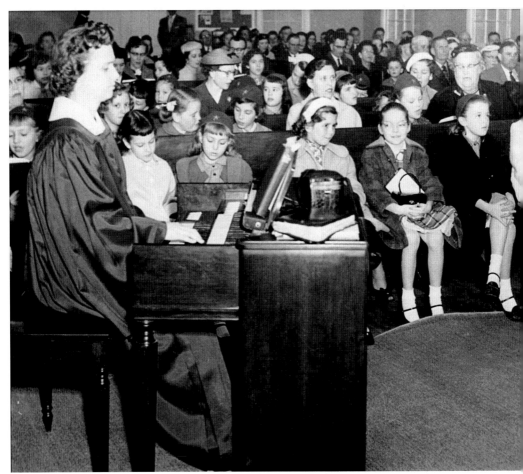

this page, top: Glad Tidings Assembly of God, Dunn, NC; *this page, above:* Eleanor playing the organ at Glad Tidings; *facing page, top:* Big crowds gathered at Glad Tidings; *facing page, bottom:* Robert, Eleanor, Paul, and Phyllis in Dunn, c. 1957

The Palmer family, Lee's Summit, MO, 1961

above: Interior of First Assembly of God, Lee's Summit, upon the Palmers' arrival in August, 1959; *right:* The Palmer family, Lee's Summit, c. 1966; *below:* First Assembly of God, Lee's Summit, 1970

facing page, top: First Pentecostal Assembly of God, Ottumwa, IA, c. 1972; *facing page, bottom right:* Eleanor preparing for choir rehearsal; *facing page, bottom left:* Robert in his office in Ottumwa, IA; *this page, clockwise from top, left:* Paul as a freshman Tuba major at Oral Roberts University, 1968; First Pentecostal Assembly of God, Ottumwa; Phyllis in junior high school in Ottumwa, c. 1970; *below:* Pastor Robert Palmer and the "Revival Hour Broadcast" on the radio in Ottumwa

above, left: Rick and Phyllis Comstock's wedding at Craig Chapel, Bethany Bible College, Scotts Valley, CA, 1975; *above, right:* Paul and Cheryl Palmer's wedding at the Crystal Cathedral, Garden Grove, CA, 1983; *right:* The Palmer family siblings: Robert, Dwight, Leonard and Margaret, San Jose, CA, 1986; *below:* The Gardner family: Virginia, Charles, Vera (mother), Leonard, Eleanor, and Jack, c. mid-1980s

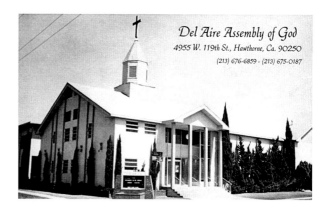

clockwise from top, right: Del Aire Assembly of God, Hawthorne, CA; First Assembly of God, Santa Maria, CA, before the new complex was built; Robert and Eleanor, Hawthorne, CA, c. 1975; *below:* The Pacific Christian Center campus with six buildings including the 999-seat sanctuary, Santa Maria, CA, 2017

clockwise from top, left: Eleanor and Robert at the Great Pyramids of Giza, Egypt, mid-1990s; Robert preaching in Indonesia with an interpreter, 1990; Missionaries Terry and Lila Townsend, their local pastor Suwandoko Roslim and his wife Emma, Eleanor and Robert, in Indonesia, 1990

left: The Palmer family: Eleanor and Robert with Paul and Cheryl; *above:* Paul (far right) and Cheryl (second from left) with their son Mike McIntyre and daughter Amy; *below:* Paul and Cheryl's son Mike and his wife Trish (center back); Robert and Eleanor's great-grandchildren, far left: Christina, far right: Justin, front: Joseph and James

clockwise from top, left: The Comstock family: Rick and Phyllis, their son Chris and his wife Cata, Eleanor and Robert; Rick and Phyllis' son Casey and his wife Theresa; Robert and Eleanor's great-granddaughters Lily Kate and Maddy Beth, daughters of Casey and Theresa

CHAPTER 14

⟡

The Call From California

I really enjoyed our ministry in Ottumwa and rejoiced in what God did during the four-and-a-half years we were there. Then one day, a phone call came to me at the office from Rev. Don Bibler, the Pastor in Hawthorne, California, at Del Aire Assembly of God. He introduced himself and then said, "I hear you want to move to California."

"Where did you hear that?"

"I saw your brother at the District Council, and he said you'd like to move out here." Pastor Bibler continued saying, "I'm moving to another church and want to be certain that a good man comes here when I leave."

He wanted us to come that weekend, but that was not possible for a number of reasons. I told him we would think and pray about it, and that we'd also like to talk with the Del Aire

97

church board by phone and learn more about the church.

Because Phyllis was at Bethany and Paul worked in North Hollywood, we, but especially Eleanor, prayed that the Lord would let us come to California in His time. Was this His time? That was the big question.

As we prayed about it and talked with the board members from Hawthorne, we decided that we would be willing to make the trip and preach for them. I informed the official board in the Ottumwa church about the call from California and that we accepted an invitation from the Hawthorne church to go to preach for them.

Colleen Guinn, a missionary to India from the Ottumwa Church, was home on furlough and was available to be the speaker while we were absent. More than 400 people were present that Sunday in the service, and a tremendous missionary offering was received.

Additionally, we learned about a surprising comment made that morning by the board member directing the service. In announcing our absence, he said, "I'm sure you notice that the Palmers are absent this morning. They're in California as candidates for another church."

That's definitely not what I wanted shared that morning. So, we made our decision to announce our resignation the following Sunday to a congregation who already knew we were leaving soon. It's not easy to leave a people whom you love; nor is it easy for a church to lose a pastor who's ministered faithfully to them.

However, it was the will of God for us to make the move to California. The remaining few weeks in the church at

Ottumwa passed by, and I preached my final sermon the last Sunday of May 1975.

CHAPTER 15

✣

*Hawthorne, California,
and Del Aire Assembly of God*

When Eleanor and I left Ottumwa, we drove to Springfield to spend the night with Eleanor's family. It was always good to see "Mom" Gardner and Eleanor's sister, Virginia. Eleanor's Dad had passed away several years before while we were in Lee's Summit. The following day, we started our trip to California excited, expectant, and wondering what we'd find ahead of us. We knew this move was like previous ones we'd made—God was in it, and we were ready for the challenges we'd face.

As we drove along the highways heading out West, we contemplated the differences that we'd find in the people in California from the Midwest. An interesting thing to note: We found people the same everywhere. As the song says "People Need The Lord."

Two of the men from Hawthorne Del Aire Assembly of God came to Ottumwa to drive our load of furniture to Redondo Beach, California. They got to Redondo Beach before we did. Some of the ladies had unpacked everything and put it in place in the apartment the church rented for us. That was such a blessing. They really did a good job to arrange the furniture in the apartment, and we felt so comfortable when we arrived. We quickly felt at home both in the area and particularly in the Del Aire church.

Once we drove west in 1975, we never drove back east again. We have found that it is more reasonable to fly rather than spend so many days and nights on the way with the cost of accommodations, gasoline, and meals. "Fly and Take Two Weeks of Vacation in One Week" became our motto. Of course if you like to drive hundreds of miles and see all the scenery, go ahead.

At Del Aire Assembly, we followed a man, Don Bibler, who was pastor for sixteen years and was well-liked by the people. He was full of enthusiasm, a hard worker, and a very strong leader. In addition, Don and his wife, LaBerta, were outstanding musicians. We were totally different people from the Biblers in our modus operandi, however, we had a call from God and the church to be there. Del Aire Assembly was so well organized that at first Eleanor didn't feel there was much for her to do in the congregation. Soon, though, she found plenty to do. Eleanor shared playing the organ with one of the fine young men of the congregation who played very well. She was also involved in the women's ministry, choir, and teaching.

A funny thing happened to me about two weeks after we

came to the church. Phyllis and Rick came down for Father's Day, and I went to the airport to pick them up. I started from the church, got on the 405 Freeway at Imperial Boulevard, and headed north toward Century Boulevard. I found there was no exit to Century and had to drive on. I then turned around and, for some reason, couldn't exit from the south either. I made about two or three runs until I realized that I had to get on a side street if I wanted to get to the airport from the church. By the time I realized what to do, people at the church had sent someone to find me. Phyllis and Rick also wondered where I was and thought I'd forgotten to collect them. I finally made it and the service continued. Sometimes, you have to learn how streets are arranged.

Our friends, Willard and Doris Tyndall from North Carolina, were there on that day, too, so Eleanor fixed a turkey and all the trimmings. Unfortunately, the oven hadn't worked as well as she had expected, and the turkey was not cooked all the way through. Eleanor trimmed meat from the outside to get something for us to eat, then she put the rest of the bird in the oven to finish cooking. It was not funny to her, but the meal was good, and the fellowship, even more wonderful. That was the first time we met Rick Comstock, our future son-in-law.

Eleanor and I found the church in Hawthorne to be doing a good work for the Lord. We tried to build on the foundation already laid. The people's hearts were open and they were ready for anything. Bus ministry was a big thing in 1975, and Del Aire was very involved in this endeavor with at least three buses, including a Trailways diesel. We found Californians as dedicated to the Lord's work as any we'd ever known. A relaxed atmosphere was in the church. There were things done in making announcements that we'd never seen before such as riding tricycles down the aisle and announcing engagements dynamically. Nothing seemed out of order, but just happy and light.

Young and old were united as a family and were very friendly to all and open to all. The bus ministry brought in many children who'd never been to Sunday School, so some things happened unexpectedly. Many of those kids who rode the buses went on to serve the Lord. The labor was not in vain. And the youth and children were also involved in what was going on for God.

One of the great missionary programs of the church was "Thanks By Giving." This was done to help a new or struggling church at Thanksgiving time. The board and committee investigated a church in the Los Angeles area that had some financial needs, or a building need, or pastoral family needs. The pastor and his wife and family members were invited to be present at Del Aire the Sunday before Thanksgiving. A Christmas tree was up, and gifts for all members of the family were given, and a sizeable cash offering was presented to the pastor for the special need of their church. It was always an exciting time for the Del Aire congregation, as well as for the chosen church and pastor's family.

I remember that one time a school bus was all fixed up and painted with the church's name and address at Goleta on it. Another time, we purchased all of the roofing materials, and then some of us helped to put up the shingles on the roof, as well as giving gifts to the pastor and family. The people at Del Aire were a loving and giving people.

Eleanor and I became Californians immediately. Del Aire Assembly was a good place to be introduced to California culture, and we enjoyed it and loved the ministry there right from the outset. We bought a house in Hawthorne, which turned out to be a great investment. We sold it when we moved to Santa Maria, and that helped us greatly.

We were always involved in the AG Districts where we've lived and, in Hawthorne, I was asked by T.C. Cunningham, the Assistant Superintendent, to serve on the World Missions Committee. I enjoyed being a part of that committee as it gave me something to do with missions. Eleanor and I have always had a vision that is worldwide, not just local. It also brought us into contact with others in leadership in the district. We were also participants in the work of God and to the leaders in the Assemblies of God.

While in Hawthorne, we discovered that more classroom space was needed. We got together with volunteer labor that worked regularly every week and built a two-story addition to the fellowship hall. This provided several new classrooms and restrooms. It was a fine addition to the buildings and has continued to be of service to the church.

We were so thankful for the qualified men who gave so freely of their time to offer advice and to provide labor to build the building that was sorely needed. Without the dedicated lay people in our churches, the tasks would have been impossible.

In all of the churches where we served as pastors, there were always people who "have addicted themselves to the ministry of the saints," *(I Corinthians 16:15, King James Version)*. Whether it was visitation, teaching, ministry to the sick and infirmed, preparation of food for the sick, building of new buildings, cleanup, preparation of communion, or bus ministry, without those who were in fact "addicted to the tasks," God's work would be undone. In all the places where we were privileged to be the pastor, we were blessed to have such people in the congregation.

Even though we enjoyed our ministry in Hawthorne, and people were being saved, and the church grew in every way, we started to feel that we might be getting ready to make a move as God directed. We began to pray that if the Lord wanted us to move, He'd open the door for us. When we went someplace to pastor, we weren't constantly looking for somewhere else to go. However, we tried to be sensitive to what the Lord might be looking to teach us. For that reason, we prayed for the Lord to direct our paths in His will and in His time.

In those days, in a church the size of Del Aire AG, visitors were still being publicly introduced. One Sunday morning in Hawthorne, I noticed that one of the visitor's cards was from David and Becky Franco from Santa Maria. As I viewed the card before I introduced them, I thought briefly, *Is he a deacon from Santa Maria First Assembly?*

Following the service, I greeted the people in the foyer and the Francos came through the line, after which they remained to the side. When everyone else had left, the Francos approached me again and asked me some questions. They said that, although they were not there in an official capacity, we had been recommended to them as a possible pastoral candidate. They came to see the church and to hear me preach.

Becky explained to me that her brother had, in fact, rented

the parsonage owned by the church. He and his wife had come to me for counseling while they were separated and I had helped them get back together, so they recommended that the Francos should come to see for themselves.

David asked me for a resume, but I told him mine was not updated—that I didn't keep it up-to-date. When I got home, I told Eleanor and she advised, "You should at least honor his request for a resume."

On Tuesday afternoon after everyone left the office, I made the updates and sent it on to David in Santa Maria. The next Monday, I received a call requesting us to come for an interview. We went to Santa Maria, were interviewed by the board, and they invited us to be candidates for pastor.

We told the board in Santa Maria that we couldn't come to candidate until after the Bentleys had returned from a trip to Europe. They'd been so good to us and supported us the five-and-a-quarter years we had been in Hawthorne. Pat was my secretary and office manager; Glen was a deacon who led the building program, and he was also our worship leader. I felt I owed it to Pat and Glen to let them know what was going on before going to candidate and/or resigning as pastor.

In the weeks following the Francos' visit, all but one of the board members came down to Hawthorne to meet us and to hear me preach. A couple of kids, one from the bus ministry and another from a family in the church, were in a fight on the lawn. One of the men from Santa Maria had to separate them. We thought they wouldn't want us to come after that, but it didn't seem to bother them at all.

Following the Bentleys' return, we went over to their house

and told them what was happening, and that we were going up to Santa Maria to preach and to be voted on. They were not happy about the news, but even so they remained good friends. Every church would be blessed to have people in it like Glen and Pat Bentley.

Prior to our going up to candidate at Santa Maria, I also summoned the official board together to inform them of the call we'd received, and that we would be going to preach soon. It's not easy for churches, nor for pastors, to go through the procedure of electing a pastor.

Eleanor and I went to Santa Maria for a weekend of preaching, singing, organ playing, meeting the congregation, and being voted on. On Sunday night following the service, the congregational meeting was held, a vote was taken, and we were elected to be the pastors of First Assembly of God of Santa Maria. I always had mixed feelings when we left a church because the people in most instances have been faithful in their support of us as their pastor, and this time was no different. Eleanor and I love people and have many friends in every place where we were the pastors.

The people of Hawthorne Del Aire Assembly were ideal to welcome us from the Midwest to California. Without a doubt, they were the most able and willing to adjust to different types of preachers than we'd ever known. Each pastor they'd had over the past 39 years was so different from the previous, however, they adjusted to us well. It was not easy to leave them after only a little more than five years, but we heard the call.

And God did it.

CHAPTER 16

Dirt and Dreams:
Santa Maria & We Build

No one really knows what condition a church is in until he's there for a time. You can tell by the atmosphere and the worship service whether or not there is unity in the body. However, there are always things which are hidden or that may not be visible to everyone. There were a lot of disappointed people in Santa Maria when we arrived—but not because we came. Several years of bad things had taken place in the preceding years under different leadership.

It was hard to get the people to begin to worship. Amens were not heard too regularly, but still God began to work in the midst. The church in Santa Maria had a "core group" of people who stood with one another and their pastor to pray, to give, and to keep the congregation together. When we arrived in 1980, about 130 people attended the church. There were about 33 students enrolled in the elementary school K-2, plus a preschool that was losing money. So our work had been laid out for us, and that work was to see the restoration of a good church returned to its place of ministry in the city.

At the time, Terry and Lila Townsend were full-time youth pastors, Glen Liming was the part-time assistant minister and visitation minister, and Lynn Rogers was the part-time music director. Dorothy Liming was secretary in the office. Edith Vawter was the Sunday School superintendent and bookkeeper for the church and school, as well as a teacher and principal of Pacific Christian School. These great people worked so well with Eleanor and me, and we began to see the church and school grow. It takes more than a pastor and his wife to accomplish what needs to be done to grow a church.

Almost immediately, the Lord began moving. Attendance began to increase in the services, and finances began to increase. It was exciting to see what the Lord was doing among us. A spiritual revival took place before our eyes. It wasn't long before we added another morning service. For seven years, we had two morning services with Sunday School in between. We also had a Sunday night service and Wednesday night activities for adults, children, and youth. I spoke at most of the services as well as on the daily radio broadcast, "The Pastor's Call."

After a little more than a year, I was also chosen to be the Presbyter for the North Coast Section. We were a very busy couple. Eleanor, as usual, was my organist for most of the time we were pastors. I am so thankful for the help she was to me for all of these 67 years. Without her, I might still be working in the courthouse in Galena, Missouri.

Eleanor's talents contributed so much to whatever success we've had in the ministry. We were exceedingly busy for the nearly twelve years that we were the senior pastors in Santa Maria. I was Presbyter for the North Coast Section and on the Board of Southern California College, now Vanguard University. I also served for a number of years as one of the regional Executive Presbyters of the Southern California District.

The Pacific Christian School (PCS) began to grow. A new grade was started every year to accommodate those who attended. Sunshine Corner Preschool also began to grow and to prosper as faithful leaders and teachers became a part of the process. At first, there were some difficulties between the Sunday School teachers and the PCS teachers concerning the multiple use of the classrooms. As the years passed, more and more parents became a part of the church, and most of the problems ceased. Again, good lay leadership had a lot to do with the growth of both schools.

As PCS began to grow, more classroom space was needed, and rooms were enlarged in the second story of the preschool building through the removal of some partitions. This was all done with the approval of the City of Santa Maria. I personally went to the Building & Safety Division and asked for advice and direction on how to proceed, and no difficulty was experienced. They were most helpful. I learned valuable lessons working with the City in this project. It was always a good idea to consult with City officials when trying to do something for the church that involves anything about building.

With the growth of the church and school, we became aware that we needed to relocate or expand in our present location, so we began looking at the possibilities at hand for expansion. The plot plan for the church showed another sanctuary between the church building and one of the present Sunday School buildings, which would about double the size of the original sanctuary.

When we first got to Santa Maria, I had heard that Valley Hospital was interested in buying the church property for expansion of their facilities and parking needs. Since it was now the appropriate time, I made an appointment with the director of the hospital to see if they were truly interested in our property and buildings. He didn't act as though they were interested any longer, so we put it from our minds and went to Florida for a vacation. While there, we received a call from the church that the hospital was, indeed, interested and for me to go to see the director when we returned. This was about 1985, and we began discussions in earnest then.

In the meantime, one of our deacons who was also a realtor, Bob Easterday, had heard that the property where the church and school are now located might be available. It was twelve-and-a-half acres, a prime location just off Highway 101. After discussions, the hospital offered to buy the Stowell Road property for $1,700,000.00 giving us three years of occupancy while new facilities were being bought and built and, in addition, paid us 12% interest on a large part of the purchase price.

Negotiations to purchase the new property for a total sum of $700,000.00 contained a provision that we must receive a conditional use permit to build a church on the property to complete the transaction. We had three years to obtain the conditional use permit, building plans, building permits and a host of other requirements to be ready for the schools to open, and the church's auditorium to be ready to move into. The Minister's Benefit Association (MBA) agreed to loan us the 2,000,000.00 needed to finance the project. We had several business meetings to put to a vote: sell the old Church, purchase the new property, hire an architect, and hire a contractor to construct the buildings. In each of the five or six polls of the congregation, there were nine negative votes cast, but these people, whomever they were, did not oppose what the overwhelming majority of the membership had decided.

We had to get authorization to borrow an additional $850,000.00. When this final vote was taken, it was 100% in favor. Praise God for such unity in the body of believers at First Assembly of God. These people were indeed people of "much faith" in God, in their board members, and in us as pastors. With each successive positive vote, it reinforced that what we were doing was what God wanted the church to do. The Ministers Benefit Association in Springfield, Missouri loaned us a total of $2,850,000.00. This retirement fund was comprised of money sent in to the MBA for all of the Assemblies of God ministers who wished to participate. Each church was encouraged to pay a percentage of their pastor's salary, and the pastor also paid a matching amount, or more, to this retirement fund. Many of the new Assemblies of God church buildings in the United States borrowed money to construct much-needed buildings.

Because we had heard that the Orcutt Town Board refused the previous owner's building plans, Bob Easterday and I took large placards showing the neighbors what we intended to build on the property. We needed approvals from both the Orcutt Town Board and the County Board of Architectural Review in Santa Barbara. The architect from Wichita and I made a number of trips to Santa Barbara before their permission was granted. Once this approval was obtained, the final building plans had to pass through the County Building Department, all of which had to be accomplished before the actual building process commenced. There were about eighteen departments that had to sign off on the building when it was completed.

One day during the early stages of the building project, T. Ray Rachels, then District Superintendent for the Southern California District Council of the Assemblies of God, stopped by to see all that was happening. I believe the concrete had been poured for the foundation and floor of the sanctuary, but there was still much to be done and dirt was everywhere.

Ray walked with me as I explained where the various rooms—choir room, classrooms, restrooms, and storage— would be located in the completed building, as well as how the wide hallway would encircle the building and give access to the rooms without passing through the sanctuary. When he returned home that night, he told his wife, Judy, and his young daughter, Heather, of his visit to the proposed building and the mounds of dirt around it. With great wisdom that belied her age, Heather said, "Daddy, it was just dirt and dreams that you saw, dirt and dreams." How true that was.

With a formidable task ahead, the Lord was with us, and we were able to get through the County of Santa Barbara permitting process and build six buildings in only three years. Thanks be to God, and to the people of God who worked with us and gave sacrificially to see a complex of buildings second to none in the area.

While pastoring, for years I instructed my board members not to surprise me at meetings with new items for the agenda, but rather to inform me in advance since many issues could be settled in a few minutes. The board in Santa Maria was very good at following instructions. One night, though, as I adjourned the meeting, Glen Liming spoke up and said, "Pastor, we have met and have spoken to a number of people …"

I thought, *What is going on here?*

"We all want to name the Fellowship Hall 'Palmer Hall,'" continued Glen.

That was a very gracious thing for them to do that night. Eleanor and I are grateful for that generous expression of love and respect.

Special thanks to Mr. Toru Miyoshi, Santa Barbara County Supervisor (retired), and to Mr. Harrell Fletcher, former board member of Santa Barbara County Supervisors (now deceased) who helped us so much in seeing that the county worked with us on the project. Former pastor Ernie Kumpe was asked by the district to assist the official board and me in assuring that things were done properly. His help was invaluable—especially in working with the contractors who performed the work. We were able to meet our time schedule and occupy the buildings in time for PCS to start in September. Our first services in the church were held on October 14, 1989.

Plans for the five buildings for the PCS Preschool and Elementary K-6 were all designed with the ages of the children in mind. A member of the congregation, Roy Thorpe, Jr. (now deceased), drew the exterior appearance of the school buildings as well as the classroom interiors. His expertise and good relationships with the county helped to get those five buildings accepted with the county. Doug Pike, principal of PCS designed all of the interiors of the classrooms for the teachers and pupils. Countertops and desks were at the level of each age. Even the toilets were made to the size of the children who would use them. Doug did an outstanding job.

When completed, PCS had the best school buildings in Santa Maria. The school has continued its excellence to this day. About 450 children and adults are on the grounds every weekday of the school year. The classrooms around the sanctuary were in use by the 6th–8th junior high classes until the 2016 school year, at which time the 7th and 8th grades were concluded. Many parents and teachers are also attending services at PCS and are a vital part of the church.

And God did it.

It was my desire that when the church was built, it would be the "meeting house" for the community. On the first Sunday night that we were in the new building, the ladies from Teen Challenge in Ventura attended. On the first Friday or Saturday night, the Santa Maria Symphony Orchestra began offering their quarterly presentations in the auditorium, which continued for a few years. There were many prominent people from Santa Maria whose memorial services were held there.

Other citywide-type services also met there throughout the years. So, my dreams of establishing a "meeting place" for the people came to pass.

Eleanor and I will never forget the first services held in the new building in October of 1989. The new sanctuary was so much larger than the original sanctuary on Stowell Road, which seated about 230 with the balcony and side room. Its total capacity was 999. If it seated 1,000 or more the building restrictions would have been even greater. It was so thrilling for the trumpet and trombone fanfare to sound; then the choir marched in singing the chorus "All Hail, King Jesus." I can almost sense the excitement today that we felt on that morning as they marched in singing.

We had decided to have a caravan from Stowell Road, a ribbon cutting and cornerstone-laying ceremony, as well as the regular service that morning.

I knew there would be a large crowd with many visitors, and I wondered, *How will we ever register all the people?* Then the Lord gave me an idea and I knew what to do. I had enough clipboards available with a place for people to sign their names, addresses, and phone numbers. Announcements were made that all who signed the clipboards would have their names placed in the cornerstone being installed at the close of the service. The clipboards were passed throughout the entire congregation, and 630 names were signed. Copies were made and, at the close of the service, those names were put in the cornerstone. Someday, they may be removed for another generation to see. That gave us a fairly accurate number of those who were present for the very first service in the new sanctuary. It was an exciting day for the congregation as a new phase of ministry began in the new church building.

And God did it.

I cannot say enough about the wonderful members of First Assembly of God who stood together through the three years of planning, meeting with county boards, giving sacrificially, supporting us as pastors, and voting on various items that were necessary. Even with changes in board member personnel, a continued unity of purpose was evident. The church sanctuary building was more than four times larger than the old sanctuary on Stowell Road, so it took some adjusting for everyone to adapt to it. However, most of the congregation were thrilled to be in our new location.

When it opened, the church became the largest seated church building in Santa Maria. Thank God for the people of vision who joined together with us to take a giant step of faith to buy the property and to build the first six buildings. It's still paying off today. The current pastor, Rick Bloom, recounts this story:

> *When I came to PCC, a huge debt remained on the church campus. There were five years between our tenures as pastors. The board initiated a debt retirement program, which authorized all Christmas, Easter, and fifth-Sunday offerings to pay down the debt on the principal mortgage. Through these efforts, we retired all except for the last $728,000.00.*
>
> *Segue to the night of March 31, 2008. Bob and I were sitting at a basketball game and he asked, "What was the largest*

contribution you have ever received?"

I gave him a number.

"What would you do if someone came in and said that they wanted to pay off the mortgage?"

I'm not even sure I had an answer, but I was about to find out.

The very next day, April 1, 2008, I was called to the home of a humble young man, new to our church. Right then and there he graciously handed me a cashier's check for $850,000.00 and said, "Retire the debt."

I was overwhelmed and contacted Pastor Palmer without delay. He wept with joy when I told him what happened. I truly believe his question the previous night was prophetic.

Today, PCC has powerful ministries that we can finance, including the largest feeding program in Santa Barbara County known as "Angel Food," a sidewalk Sunday School for inner city kids, a recovery program, and many more ministries. I attribute much of this to the vision, dreams, and hard work of the Palmers.

They will always be Heroes of the Faith in my book.

Through the ministry of Pastor Rick Bloom, the church is growing numerically, financially and spiritually—in an effort to reach hundreds of people in this area and to the ends of the earth through missionary giving—both here and abroad.

And God did it.

From the time we moved to the new location on Santa Maria

Way, the congregation began to grow. There were fresh opportunities to reach new people through the ministry of Pacific Christian School, as well as through the regular church services. We were now able to have one Sunday morning service with Sunday School before. It seemed the right thing to do since we had more than enough room for everyone who had attended in the two services in the old church.

This was good for most of us. Unfortunately, there were some who were hindered from coming Sunday morning due to work schedules. However, I say "Thank God" that two services were needed again to accommodate those who attended on Sunday mornings. As the weeks, months and years have passed, the congregation began to grow and grow, with more and more souls being saved and filled with the Holy Spirit. Many new people became members of the church and participated in the innovation that took place. As parents became aware of the excellent teachers and classrooms, the Pacific Christian School began to grow also in its new facilities.

And God did it.

CHAPTER 17

✧

There's No Such Thing as an Ex-Pastor

From the time when we were in our twenties and assistant pastors at Bethel Temple in St. Louis, Eleanor and I had talked about what it would be like when we were older. We had decided that if at all possible, we'd retire from the pressures of being pastors of a church when we became the age of 65. This was not because we no longer felt the call to the ministry, but possibly we could do something else as we grew older. As we prayed and thought of the work that needed to be done for the future of the church in Santa Maria, we decided that after reaching 65 we should consider resigning from being the pastor of the church which we loved so dearly and had led the congregation into building.

In May of 1992, we presented our resignation to the official board and church, to be effective when a new pastor was elected. We really didn't know what our next move would be. We jokingly thought we might need to rent out our house fully furnished and go overseas and wash dishes or something for the Lord there.

When Pastor Ernie Kumpe learned of our resignation, he came by one day and asked me to go with him to visit some churches down in the Central Section—Santa Barbara and Ventura—areas. While travelling, he asked me if I would be interested in doing the work he had been doing for the Southern California District as an Area Director for District Affiliated Churches. He said he would be leaving that ministry to go back on staff at Visalia as they planned to build there.

I replied that I'd definitely be interested in doing that. A little later I received a call from our District Superintendent, Ray Rachels, inviting me to become Area Director for 50 Churches from the North at San Miguel and Shandon and along the coast in six sections as far south as Orange County and the Foothill sections. Of course, this was a part-time position, so my main task was to bring encouragement and help to the pastors and churches to whom I would minister. It presented us with a small monthly honorarium, plus mileage and other expenses as needed. This was another evident leading of the Lord.

For the next twenty-two-and-a-half years, I served in that position. It was such a privilege for us to work with the pastors and boards of these mostly smaller and/or troubled churches that needed help in so many areas, including finances; and also to provide advice in matters relating to other business aspects of ministry. These were important things that were sometimes neglected. I was also able to represent a given church to the

District Officials when said church needed financial aid for some important project.

Several of us retired or semi-retired ministers became Area Directors across the district, and we worked with more than 200 district area churches and pastors. We conducted business meetings, preached for them, recommended ministers to be pastors of a church, offered advice, helped solve problems and, sometimes, recommended that a change be made for the benefit of the church and/or the pastor. In my opinion, it was a very good program that someone needed to do. I met with the pastors on a regular basis in sectional meetings as well as private meetings.

I was also a member of the board of the churches for whom I served. In one given year, I attended 92 board meetings.

Each pastor was instructed to turn in a monthly report of all activities, including attendance and finances. We had a yearly evaluation time where their goals and aspirations were presented. Some very positive things happened in these churches as a result of the regular oversight provided by the Area/Field Directors who, for more than 20 years, maintained this ministry. In December two years ago, some changes were made in the network, and so we are now back home most of the time.

In the years since we left Santa Maria First Assembly of God in 1992, the name of the church was changed to Pacific Christian Center, which encompasses the Pacific Christian Preschool and Pacific Christian Elementary School, as well as the Church. Pacific Christian Center of Santa Maria is known throughout Southern California as an "anchor church" where great things are happening.

Our dream came true. People are being saved week by week, and more than 170 were baptized in water in recent years. Attendance continues to grow, and ministries have been started here that affect the whole city. The Angel Food Ministry provides groceries to hundreds of people each week. Many people come each Friday night for Celebrate Recovery. God is being glorified through the efforts of the people of PCC. The church and school are well known and respected in the whole area. On an average day, about 450 people are on the campus, including students and teachers and helpers. Praise be to God.

And God did it.

The current pastor, Rick Bloom of Pacific Christian Center, has asked us as "Pastors Emeritus" to participate on Wednesday nights by leading worship with Eleanor playing the organ. I've also spoken a number of times in the past several years in the church. It is so thrilling for Eleanor and me to see how the church has grown numerically, financially, and spiritually during the years of the ministry of Pastor Bloom and Jan, while she lived. Not too many people were afforded the opportunity to attend the church they formerly pastored. In these years of semi-retirement—and now being truly retired—we've been blessed by being able to attend Pacific Christian Center and fellowship with so many that we've known throughout the years.

And God did it.

CHAPTER 18

Whitened Fields

During the years that I was Presbyter, Executive Presbyter and Area/Field Director, I was given the privilege to preach in every church in the North Coast Section except Paso Robles. I was also asked to preach in many of the churches in the other five sections of Southern California in which we worked. God has been so good to Eleanor and me to enable us to spend so much of our time in active service for the Lord— even after we reached retirement age. We never dreamed when we were young that we'd ever have been given the opportunities afforded to us during these 67 years of our lives together in ministry.

As I have often said, "I asked the Lord to give me a wife who could play the piano, sing alto, and love me." He surely answered my prayers in an abundant manner. Eleanor has been my pianist and organist for all of these 67 years. She has always been ready to play at a moment's notice. Plus, she's a great housekeeper, decorator, organizer, and teacher. Eleanor has traveled with me almost constantly since my retirement from being a pastor in 1992. We've been to every state in the USA and have visited and preached across the nation and in many places around the world. Praise Be to God.

And God did it.

The following is a list of countries that we have visited in these years: Aruba, Australia, Austria, The Bahamas, Barbados, Belgium, Bermuda, Brazil, Canada, Canary Islands, China, Costa Rica, Czech Republic, Egypt, England, France, Germany, Greece, Hong Kong, Hungary, Indonesia, Ireland, Israel, Italy, Japan, Jordan, Korea, Lebanon, Lichtenstein, Mexico, the Netherlands, New Zealand, Norway, Panama, Philippine Islands, Poland, Principality of Monaco, Puerto Rico, Russia, Spain, Scotland, Singapore, Switzerland, Thailand, Trinidad and Tobago, Ukraine, and Wales.

Some of these were places of ministry, but some we just visited on cruises or bus tours or on our own. We taught for three or four weeks each in Poland, Ukraine, and Austria, as well as preaching two weeks nightly in the Philippine Islands and two weeks in Brazil. Teaching in most foreign lands is through an interpreter, but in the Philippines we spoke in English because they almost all learn English in their schools.

And God did it.

It's interesting how we became Bible schoolteachers in other countries. Eleanor and I were with Fred Cotttriel, our former District Superintendent, and his wife, Lucille, eating at a restaurant when Fred suddenly said, "I need someone to teach in the Bible School in Poland. I don't know who to get to do this."

Immediately, Eleanor spoke up and said, "Bob, you could do this."

"Yes, you can do it," Fred agreed.

That's how we began some overseas teaching in Bible colleges in at least three countries. We went to Poland shortly after the Iron Curtain came down. That was a great experience for us. I taught through an interpreter to a group of young people who were destined to be an influence in that poor country. We also went to Ukraine and taught at the Kiev Regional Bible College for three or four weeks. Being in these countries gave us a much greater burden for those who were suppressed for so long under Communist leaders.

Our last trip to teach was with Fred Cottriel in Vienna, Austria, at the seminary there. What a privilege to share teaching responsibilities with Fred. He was well known in most of the European countries because he and Lucille had been missionaries prior to their pastorate in Bakersfield and before he became District Superintendent of Southern California. We also went to Budapest, Hungary, where we met the wife of a missionary.

After becoming involved in this way, we went to Brazil for two weeks of meetings for a large church that had many smaller satellite churches under the direction of its pastor. We enjoyed so much being in the home of the pastor and traveling to several of the other churches under his direction. Each had a choir, orchestra, and good attendance the night we were guest speakers. The privilege of ministering in other countries was so good for our own growth in ministry.

And God did it.

We also spent two weeks in the Philippine Islands at the invitation of Pastor Rolando Dinglas and his wife, Purisima, who came to the states and founded Full Life Christian Assembly, a Filipino Church in Oxnard, California. We were instrumental in helping them to start the church here since I was the Executive Presbyter for the region. We ministered on Bataan primarily, and also in Manila and Cavite. Several of us also had the privilege of going to Baguio City where the Assemblies of God seminary, Asia Pacific Theological Seminary is located. John Carter was the President of the seminary, and we were also able to see one of Eleanor's former classmates, Leota Morar, who taught at the seminary. We went out to eat a genuine Mongolian dinner. It was a great meal and, since then, we have eaten a few times at a Mongolian restaurant in Ventura. The meat is all cooked in front of your eyes on a large stainless steel round grill. You should try it sometime; it's delicious.

It was an interesting trip as we all were in a pickup truck outfitted with benches and a cover over it. Because I was not feeling well, I sat in the front seat with the driver. We preached at several churches during the two weeks of our stay, and I spoke at a local Bible college one day.

We also visited an orphanage high up on a mountain that a lady from the United States had devoted her life and resources to maintaining. Thank God for lay people who are willing to dedicate themselves to going to the ends of the earth to minister to the needy. The opportunity to go overseas in ministry gave us even more of a burden to try to reach the lost all over the world. It also gave us a greater realization of what all of our missionaries face when they serve abroad.

And God did it.

One of the great experiences we had was to go to Indonesia to see Terry and Lila Townsend and their children where they taught and preached. We visited Singapore and attended Trinity Christian Centre, the great church where Naomi Dowdy was the pastor. We also saw an apartment rented by the youth pastor of the church. Sister Dowdy invited us to see a cleansing of the demon spirits, which might have been there since it was a place where the gods of the former inhabitants were kept. Each room was anointed with oil, and prayers were offered in each, as well as in the closet where the gods had been stored. It was not for show or pretense—they really prayed for the protection of the youth pastor from any evil spirits that might have stayed. In America, we're not as conscious of the way people in other countries are oppressed by the devil. It was an eye-opening experience.

We were invited to stay in the apartment of Bill and Jeanette Robertson, our former District Superintendent and his wife, who became missionaries to Singapore. They had arranged for their driver to take us around Singapore. It was such a wonderful gift that they offered up their home to us while they were in the United States on furlough. Singapore was such a beautiful and well-maintained place. It would do our city planners good to go over and see what they've done and to take notes. Some of their requirements were very stringent—people did not throw trash around on the streets and chewing gum was forbidden. We've never visited a cleaner city than Singapore.

In Indonesia, there were also many evidences of the power of the devil and the worship of idols. On our way to the Townsend's apartment, a naked man ran down the street. It didn't take long to realize we were in a different culture and facing the challenges of a heathen society. Also, in these Eastern countries, there are idols; altars where food is laid out for their ancestors and gods.

We had the privilege to preach at the large church in Jakarta where hundreds of people gather each Sunday to worship Jesus Christ. While there, the Townsends, Eleanor and I went over to Bali, another island that is well known as a vacation destination. There is a wonderful beach, and the water was so nice and warm to swim in. We really enjoyed our visit there.

We also were privileged to visit missionaries Jim and Karla Gutel in Thailand. They had an apartment above their garage, which was so convenient. It gave us such joy to visit these missionaries who, to this day, are good friends as they continue ministry in the SoCal Network with the SoCal School of Ministry. This is a very vital part of the SoCal Network as many people who apply for credentials with the Assemblies of God get their training through this school of ministry. I was given the opportunity to speak to the church and Bible College in Thailand, as well.

And God did it.

When we were appointed to be Area Directors for the Southern California District Council of the Assemblies of God (SCDC) in June of 1992, we were paid a small honorarium plus expenses. This has allowed us to minister around the world.

And God did it.

One of the best trips was to Russia when Terry and Lila Townsend lived there. Since we visited Terry and Lila in Indonesia, we decided to travel to Moscow to see them in their new location. A few months after the collapse of the Soviet Union, they started International Christian Assembly, the first English-speaking church in Moscow.

Along with Russians, many people from other nations work in Russia. They want to speak English, and some of them will seek out a church where English is spoken rather than attend a Russian-speaking church. Terry and Lila did good work for the Lord in getting this church to reach the people.

After our contact with them, Terry told Bob Mackish, the Assemblies of God lead missionary in Russia who hailed from Kansas, that we were coming.

Bob Mackish said, "Good, we'll go down to Rostov which is about 600 miles from Moscow and start a new church. Bob

Palmer can do the preaching, and we'll get a new church under way."

We flew down to Rostov on one of the Russian Aeroflot planes. The seats were broken, and the one in front of me leaned back into my lap. One lady boarded without a seat assigned and refused to get off, so they let her sit in the flight attendant's seat.

We arrived safely in Rostov and spent two nights in a really "rustic" mice-infested hotel. The windows were held shut with masking tape, so I tore through the tape with my hands and opened a window to get fresh air. The next day a dead mouse was found under the bed. Enough of that.

Bob Mackish had told me to preach for first-time decisions for Christ. He said they'd all come forward if I asked for healing, because they were all sick. The great news is that in the three services—Saturday afternoon and Sunday morning and afternoon—about 100 people of all ages came forward to accept Christ for the first time in their lives. There were old women in their babushkas and young military men. It was truly wonderful to experience what the Lord had done.

We met in what was a former Communist youth hall that had the hammer-and-sickle insignia on the inside and outside walls. Bob Mackish and the Russian brethren had planned ahead. A pastor was already appointed to begin services in the same hall on Wednesday night following the three services we had conducted. Later, Bob Mackish told us that the church grew to 700 people. Last year at the 100th Anniversary of the Assemblies of God in Springfield, we met a Russian brother who told us that the church had grown to 1,000 people and started 17 other churches in the area. Praise God for the wonders He performs.

This was, without a doubt, the greatest thrill of our ministry: to be able to speak to people with whom we never thought we'd meet. But God had other plans. Who would have thought that Russia would open to the Gospel? However, our Missions Department tells us that the door is closing and many restrictions are now being placed upon Christian outreach ministries. Since that time, a pastor in Russia was arrested for some infraction of that new law. It's really restrictive. We must pray. It may be in the United States next.

And God did it.

Epilogue

As Eleanor and I are in our ninetieth year, we move a little slower, have a few more pains and stumble sometimes, but we remain on the firing line for the Lord. At present, Eleanor still plays the organ on Wednesday nights, and I lead the the old choruses and the singing from the hymnbook.

We are so thankful for the people in each of the churches in which we were the pastors. People have been so good to us throughout the years with their prayers, financial support, cooperation and love. We both tried to be pastors to all the people, not to just a few favored ones. Of course, pastors are closer to some people because they work with them daily or they serve on church boards or school boards together or they labor together in a particular ministry that requires closer contact with the pastor. As a mother once replied when asked which child she loved the most, she said, "The one who needs me the most right now."

No matter where we were pastors, we always tried to be available when needed. The local church was our priority. Our policy was to devote ourselves to the present situation wherever we ministered.

God has been so good to us in the years we have been in the ministry. We have only been the pastors of one church to which we actually applied for the pastorate, and that was Lee's Summit, Missouri. We know that God has highly blessed us to be in ministry together for 67 years.

Thank God for His goodness and mercy that endureth forever.

"Now to Him who is able to do exceedingly abundantly above all that we ask or think, according to the power that works in us, to Him be glory in the church by Christ Jesus to all generations, forever and ever. Amen," *(Ephesians 3:20-21, New King James Version).*

And God did it.

AFTERWORD

You have now finished reading our parents' story. It is the story of two people who were faithful to their God, to each other, to their children, and to the ministry to which God had called them.

In 2002, Rick Warren wrote *The Purpose Driven Life: What on Earth Am I Here For?* The book inspired a whole generation of believers to find the answers to these two questions: Why am I here, and what is God's purpose for my life? In 1945, fifty-seven years before *Purpose* was published, our dad knew exactly why he was here and what his purpose was. He did not have an equivalent publication, unless you count the Bible. To help further identify his purpose, Dad sought wise counsel from men of God who poured themselves into the vessel that was our dad. His purpose was to preach the Gospel and make disciples of those entrusted to his care as pastor. Our mother's passion to serve God was equal to that of Dad's. Their combined passion for their purpose together, created a formidable "force" that proclaimed the good news of the gospel, and sustained them through 67 years of marriage and 72 years of ministry.

Pastor Rick Bloom, senior pastor of Pacific Christian Center, recently said, "There is no word for retirement in the Bible, it is called death." He cited the example of Abraham and Moses. Dad "retired" from active pastoral ministry, but did not end his ministry. The next 23 years were spent being a pastor to pastors. Just as Rev. Howard Osgood and Rev. Henry Hoar had done four decades earlier for him, our dad was doing the same with young pastors just starting out in ministries of their own.

Our parents' lives have been quite remarkable:

- Dad began full-time ministry 72 years ago at the age of eighteen.
- At the age of 22, they became assistant pastors in one of the largest churches in the Midwest.
- They were called to pastor the largest Assembly of God church in North Carolina when they were just 27 years old.
- At the age of 32, Dad took on not only the job of pastor, but also of general contractor, completing the building of their next church.
- They served as pastors of three other established churches in Iowa and California and saw growth in every way.

- In Santa Maria, Dad used all that he had learned in his previous 34 years of ministry. He had the vision for a new campus, led the charge, and did not give up when faced with being told "No." Dirt and dreams did, indeed, became reality with Pacific Christian Center sitting at the intersection of South Bradley Road and Santa Maria Way.

Not only were both of our parents effective ministers, they were also great parents who supported us in achieving our dreams. Some of our fondest memories are those long road trips across the United States listening to AM radio, trying to find stations that carried radio evangelist Lester Roloff or the "Back to the Bible" broadcast. Disneyland, Yellowstone Park, Yosemite, Grand Canyon, and Morehead City, North Carolina, were just a few of the many places we happily spent our family vacations.

Paul says, "They nurtured my musical aspirations. They took me to the Kansas City Public Library to listen to record albums and to check out musical scores to practice conducting at home. Knowing that I loved band music, they surprised me by taking me to hear the United States Navy Band, a concert that I remember to this day."

Phyllis says, "They supported me in my musical endeavors also, attended numerous recitals, endured school concerts and plays, and soothed my many broken hearts. They have also encouraged me in my desire to be in ministry. And, they made it possible for me to attend Bethany Bible College where I met my husband, Rick Comstock."

Music was and has always been an integral part of our parents' ministry, and it is a love and talent they have passed on to us. In fact, many of our Palmer relatives are quite musical. There is a well-known Christian song, written by Jon Mohr and popularized by Steve Green, entitled *Find Us Faithful*. You will find the lyrics on the next page. If there is anything that epitomizes the grace and decorum with which our parents have lived and conducted themselves, and their parents before them, it is this: *The heritage of faithfulness passed on through godly lives.* This is what our parents have given to us, and to our children, and to their children, too. And to the countless congregations, missions, and people with whom their lives have crossed and touched. It is our hope that their story, and their testimony, will be an inspiration not only to those who have had the privilege of knowing them, and experiencing their faithfulness firsthand, but also to those who will have found them faithful in the generations that follow.

Mom and Dad, thank you so much for being such a blessing to us, to our families, and to innumerable people throughout the world.

—Paul E. Palmer and Phyllis Palmer Comstock

Find Us Faithful

We're pilgrims on the journey of the narrow road,
And those who've gone before us line the way,
Cheering on the faithful, encouraging the weary
Their lives a stirring testament to God's sustaining grace.

Surrounded by so great a cloud of witnesses,
Let us run the race not only for the prize,
But as those who've gone before us, let us leave to those behind us,
The heritage of faithfulness passed on through godly lives.

Oh may all who come behind us find us faithful,
May the fire of our devotion light their way,
May the footprints that we leave lead them to believe,
And the lives we live inspire them to obey,
Oh may all who come behind us find us faithful.

After all our hopes and dreams have come and gone,
And our children sift through all we've left behind,
May the clues that they discover, and the memories they uncover
Become the light that leads them to the road we each must find.

Oh may all who come behind us find us faithful,

May the fire of our devotion light their way,

May the footprints that we leave lead them to believe,

And the lives we live inspire them to obey,

Oh may all who come behind us find us faithful.

Oh may all who come behind us find us faithful.

WORDS AND MUSIC BY JON MOHR